CW00493156

Loving

Female Led Relationship

Stories

Real Stories from Real People
in Loving FLRs

Compiled and Edited By

Te-Erika Patterson

ACKNOWLEDGMENTS

My most heartfelt appreciation goes out to Vince N. and the Loving FLR Community for their contributions to the collection of stories in this book. Your openness about your Loving FLRs will encourage others to experience the beauty of Loving Female Led Relationships.

Te-Erika

CONTENTS

III | Te-Erika Patterson

INTRODUCTION

Welcome to the wonderful world of Loving Female Led Relationships. I am so glad that you have decided to learn more about this exciting and wonderful relationship style. Who am I? I am Te-Erika Patterson, a Black Goddess loving life in Fort Lauderdale, Florida. I am the Publisher of LovingFLR.Com, a website that helps singles and couples create relationships that empower women.

I am also the author of *She Wants: A Loving Female Led Relationship*, *How to Love a Powerful Woman* and the *Loving Female Led Relationship COUPLES WORKBOOK*. All of these tools help couples ease into establishing a Loving Female Led Relationship (Loving FLR).

You are probably reading this book for one of two reasons. Either you have been fantasizing about establishing your very own Loving FLR or someone offered this book to you as a gift so that you can learn more about Loving FLRs. Regardless of the reason that brought you to this very moment, you are in for a treat. Before you read about the intimate details of couples in Loving FLRs from around the world, allow me to explain the basic premise of a Loving FLR.

A Loving Female Led Relationship is a committed, Loving union in which the woman's happiness, satisfaction and progress are the primary focus in the relationship. She sets specific expectations and standards for the relationship and her partner will do whatever it takes to ensure her happiness. He honors her choices. He ensures that she has everything she needs to create a wonderful life for their family. Couples involved in Loving Female Led Relationships have openly agreed that she is the leader in the relationship and he is content in his role as supporter.

This means that she accepts the responsibility to openly express what she wants from their relationship and his responsibility is to listen to her and support her desires. A Loving FLR adds peace and progress to the couple because they have established roles that they agree to abide by. She decides which duties and responsibilities he will have and he follows her direction. His goal is to help her to create her dream life. All she has to do is decide what she wants, express it to him openly and allow him to make it happen.

The biggest benefit of a Loving FLR for women is the ability to have their desires heard, respected and supported by a man who cherishes them. Have you ever wished your partner would love you in the way that you really want to be loved? In a Loving FLR the woman can explicitly tell him what she wants and he will listen and respect her wishes.

The biggest benefit of a Loving FLR for men is the ability to shed the gender roles prescribed by society and wholeheartedly worship a woman who adores them. There are a certain class of men that we call Gentleman who sincerely adore women. A Gentleman's happiness is dependent upon the woman's happiness. When she smiles, he feels like he has fulfilled his purpose in this world.

Couples in Loving FLR experience the bliss of structure, clarity, peace of mind that allows them to progress as a team with little to no conflict. When there is an established leader and supporter, the battle for power is eliminated and a couple can create a beautiful life without hindrance.

Sounds like a dream, right? Well, for the majority of readers and followers of LovingFLR.Com, this relationship style *is* a dream. The major challenge in establishing a Loving FLR is finding a partner who wants one. Most people have been entrenched in the idea that all relationships should follow the man's lead yet, there is a population of people who want to step outside of this societal expectation.

There are women who are naturally wise enough to make decisions for their relationships. These women have big dreams for their lives and want a partner who will not try to crush their dreams or compete with them for control.

There are also many men who crave the guidance of Powerful Women and want nothing more than to support and serve a woman who is equally as devoted to them yet they find that most women do not want to lead their relationship. Women fear expressing their leadership abilities due to lack confidence and the expectations from a society that has taught them that it is wrong to stand up and express their brilliance, wisdom and power.

Loving FLRs will benefit our society as a whole, eliminating discord between men and women and urging women to express their wisdom and leadership in their homes and in the world.

I have taken up the task of educating the masses about the benefits of establishing Loving FLRs. In order to help propel the concept of Loving FLRs into the mainstream I have created **Loving FLR Coaching Programs** for women, men and couples, **Loving FLR books and workbooks**, an online school called **Loving FLR Academy** that allows students to take classes at their leisure and a **Loving FLR Matchmaking Service**. Access to all of these tools and services can be found on **FLRStyle.Com**.

The stories collected in *Loving Female Led Relationship STORIES* are all true stories submitted to LovingFLR.Com by real people from all around the world. These stories have been selected and edited for clarity and consistency with our primary message. Most of the stories in this book share tales of happy Loving FLRs yet there are a few stories from singles who have experienced a Loving FLR and lost it as well as stories from those who actively yearn to create one.

Wherever you are in your journey to creating your very own Loving FLR, this book will feed your soul and offer insight into the many preferences, duties and emotions that make up Loving FLRs. No Loving FLR is the same. All women can create the exact relationship of their personal dreams with a man who has chosen to help make it happen.

I wish you the best in your journey to a Loving FLR and I invite you to subscribe to LovingFLR.Com to read the latest stories and meet others who share your passion for empowering women.

Te-Erika

FLR READER SURVEY RESULTS

These are the results from our most recent LovingFLR.Com Reader Survey which will offer insight into the demographics, preferences and attitudes of the Loving FLR Community.

- 90% of our readers are men.
- Nearly 60% of our readers are married.
- 72% of our readers do not have children in their homes.
- 22% of our readers are business owners.
- Nearly 80% of our readers believe the woman should be the authority in the relationship and the man should follow her lead.
- The majority of our readers live in the North America, followed by Europe and Australia.
- The majority of our readers are between the ages of 42-65.
- Nearly 60% of our readers have completed college and/or post graduate studies.
- 70% of our readers indicate that they are not religious.
- The majority of our readers are moderately conservative.
- Our readers indicate that the top 3 hindrances to establishing a Loving FLR are fear, lack of trust, and stigma from society.
- 60% of our readers are not involved in BDSM activities at all.
- Nearly 70% of our readers believe that women are superior to men.
- 75% of our readers do not believe that the woman should be the primary breadwinner in the relationship.

- 40% of our readers believe that they could publicly acknowledge their Loving FLRs without negative repercussions and 20% believe that they would receive positive feedback and admiration from their peers and friends if they were involved in a Loving FLR.
- 65% of our readers were not raised in a home where the woman was the leader.
- The majority of our readers believe that leadership in a Loving FLR is indicated when the woman sets the vision for the progress of the relationship and guides it.
- Nearly 80% of our readers believe that the most important factor in a Loving FLR is a woman's ability to openly express what she wants from the relationship.
- When thinking about participating in a Loving FLR, 25% of our readers report feeling *aroused* and 25% reported feeling *intrigued*.
- 37% of our readers would best describe a woman in a Loving FLR as *bossy* and 57% would best describe a man in a Loving FLR as *supportive.*
- When asked to describe the biggest indication that a couple is in a Loving FLR, 42% said that the woman in a Loving FLR is happy and confident at home and out in the world.
- The readers of LovingFLR.Com reported that the biggest benefits of being in a Loving FLR are happiness, safety, respect, contentment and clear boundaries.

SECTION 1

His Trust in Me Made Me More Confident

Can you believe that I am a 42-year-old woman and I am already retired? I have this beautiful gift because of my husband. What started as a pretty average relationship changed into a Loving FLR when he asked me to give him advice about his career. He is a smart man, but he seemed to lack motivation in the past. When I met him I was happily working in retail and he was a junior associate at his company. He had been a junior associate for many years with no desire to move up.

One day over dinner he asked me for my opinion about changing positions at his company. I was happy that he asked because I had been thinking about it for a while but I didn't want him to feel pressured by me. I told him that I thought he was too smart for his current position and that he should buy a new suit and go for a higher position immediately.

He did just as I advised and within a month he was earning significantly more than before. He was so proud and happy that he began to ask me for advice all of the time and whatever I advised, he would do. His trust in me made me more confident and I began reading more about successful people in his field, learning their techniques and offering advice even when he didn't ask.

He always followed my suggestions and he kept improving, we kept improving. He treats me as though I am his favorite mentor and I have stepped up to be the best mentor I can be.

I let him know when I thought we were ready to live together. I let him know when I thought it was time to buy a home. I even I let him know when I thought it was time for us to be married. Every time I made a suggestion, he listened. He still does. I told him that I wanted to be a house wife and retire from working and he agreed. He asked what he needed to do to make that happen and I gave him a goal for our savings account. He met that goal in a little more than a year.

I do invest a good amount of time into guiding him in his career and challenging him to be a better man. I want a fit husband. I want a savings account that is healthy. I want to always look nice and I want him to look nice too. I want to focus on our spirituality and wholeness. It does not matter what I suggest, he genuinely seems eager to try it and learn more. I don't know what I did to deserve such a man but I show him how much I appreciate him every day.

My Pleasure Comes from My Wife's Pleasure

I am 56 years old, live in Phoenix, Arizona and I am a business owner and leader of a financial services company that has about 75 employees. I believe that I am among the group of otherwise "alpha" males that are in-charge through almost every aspect of his life, except of course my marriage to my Wife. Things I enjoy are fishing, baseball and other outdoor activities with my teenage sons and my friends. I have a great relationship with all four of my children, two of which are all grown up. I am 12 years older than my beautiful wife. When we married, I was the absolute alpha, loving leader in our relationship. About four to five years ago, I asked her to join me in a Female Led Marriage and she agreed to do so.

My wife and I have always gotten along amazingly. Roughly 10 years into our loving marriage she made an off-handed comment about wondering whether or not we would have anything in common once the children left the nest. That starting me on a path to figure out the best way not to let that happen. Not to let two people that love and care for each other, suddenly find themselves feeling like strangers. I began researching and discovered the relationship benefits of a Female Led Marriage. I mustered up the courage and asked my wife to become my Goddess. Since then, our love is deep, our marriage is stronger and our future is bright.

Our Female Led Marriage has absolutely and genuinely allowed me to be able to focus all (OK, most) of my energy to providing the pleasures in life, not just sexually, to my Wife. I truly and genuinely do receive a large percentage of my pleasure from providing and witnessing my Wife's pleasure.

We have small, otherwise barely significant rituals that I must always adhere to, without being asked or told. I must have her coffee prepared for her every morning when she wakes up. Dishes. If it a dish and it needs to be washed anywhere in the house, that is my responsibility, again without being asked or told. The understanding and comfort that comes from knowing she is automatically attended to in these small ways and others is general pleasure for her, but provides a continuous source of pleasure for me.

At various times and whenever the mood strikes her, she will have me massage a part of her that is aching. Full body massages are also something she knows is at her beck and call.

My wife has little or no interest in attaining the porn-like depiction of the kind of lifestyle a Mistress Wife would lead. She enjoys being the mother of our children and attending to them in traditional motherly ways (meal preparation, laundry, keeping the house clean). After I offered my devotion to her, and asked her to lead our marriage, we talked very carefully about what we hoped to achieve. Neither of us had an interest in turning our marriage, family, standing in the community on its head in dramatic fashion. She made it clear that being the one in the house that provides the love and attention that a "typical" wife and mother would provide is what she wants. To take those things away from her so she could sit on the couch and read a book, or take tennis lessons, or go find another lover while her husband attended to the house matters, had zero appeal to her. That being said, she gets a great deal of pleasure in knowing that she alone can decide, at any given moment, what gets done by and by whom, without an ounce of debate or defiance.

I'd say her biggest source of pleasure lies in the knowledge that she is indeed a Queen in her realm, and has at her disposal a genuinely loving, completely dutiful, willing subject in her viral, masculine, strong and protective king. He is a king that is alpha in every other aspect of his life, a leader of men and women, a business owner, a mentor to many and a leader to most and an icon in the community ... strong, intelligent and honor filled. To know that she essentially owns that king, is a strong and constant source of pleasure for her.

I will do most things that society believes a true gentleman should do. I open car doors for her and if you were to observe us you'd know that this is done with intent and with service in mind. My wife will walk to the passenger side of the car and if she arrives a few seconds before I do, she will demurely stand and look at the door, knowing that I will be there to open it for her. Can she open her doors without any trouble? Of course she can, but that isn't the point. It is a matter of respect for me to be expected to open (any) doors for her. As such, it is also a subtle way for us to perhaps demonstrate to each other and the world, who is in charge of our relationship. The beautiful woman is naturally always treated well because the man that loves her genuinely gets pleasure from seeing her pampered, attended to and loved. That little smile of blissful contentment is as powerful as any drug.

Our Female Led Marriage is a private matter. Only one other person (her very best friend) knows of some of the intimate details of our lifestyle. It appears to the outside world that I am the alpha dog, I suppose on par with your typical husband in a typical marriage where you can see the love is there, but hardly ever is demonstrated. In this context, I will declare for everyone to hear how beautiful I think she is, or I will openly address her as "babydoll" or some similar loving word. During times when we are together with couple friends and others but not next to each other, I habitually make it a point to go to her, kiss her on the lips lovingly but not like a horny teenager, look her in the eye and smile before walking away. Of course it makes her happy to have her friends tell her how lucky she is to have her husband dote on her like he is still courting her, which at the end of the day, he is still courting her. He is constantly courting her.

The biggest benefit for me has been the wonderful, almost constant state of desire I have for her. As a result of our love for each other, my constant state of desire and my requirement to demonstrate my affection for her any time I feel it, our friends have all noticed that open affection. Many of her contemporaries have commented to her about wonderful it is that I am dutiful and affectionate toward her in public, and that they wished their husbands would learn from me in that regard. We make little innuendos and jokes about the ramifications for me should there be a lack of affection that go under their radar, but my Wife and I know that it is true. I am proud whenever she tells me about a friend of hers that compliments us on our obvious affection for each other.

My Wife has an incredible amount of street smarts. As such, throughout her entire life she has used those skills to navigate around/over/through things in order to obtain the things/way of life she wanted. Once she became comfortable with the knowledge that she could indeed be in control of that path, without unnecessary manipulation, her cleverness and craftiness took over and led her down the path to continued growing happiness in her life.

My advice would be to AVOID AT ALL COSTS seeking some sort of set-of-rules by others, that you may think you have to abide by in order to have a Loving FLR. It seems that most people seeking advice tend to think they need to start a conversation with "Do people usually ....?" I wish someone would've told me that it doesn't matter what most people do. Figuring out what makes her happy and making sure you keep doing it is what really matters.

My Needs Are My Husband's Priority

I am 42 years old, I live in Denver, Colorado with my husband Ray, our son Raiden and my daughter Destiny from a previous relationship. I am a Le-Vel Brand promoter, I help people live better lives with plant based vitamins. For fun I love being out and about with my family and friends. We love going to the mountains, being in nature, going to museums, amusement parks, movies, hanging out with friends, going out for drinks and dancing. I like to always be busy. My family and I are very close. We have lots of open discussions about our futures, what's going on with us, our desires, we have a judgement free home and try to keep things positive, feeling and knowing we are loved and supported is my number one priority.

I have never read anything on Female Led Relationships; I was told about this site by Te-Erika. I met her in a group that helps to empower victims and survivors of abuse. She wrote a beautiful story about me and finding happiness in a loving healthy relationship years later after leaving a severe domestic violence relationship.

I learned from her that I am now in a Loving Female Led Relationship. This relationship has been phenomenal. My needs are my husband's number one priority. I am able to lead my own life and be independent. I know he is there and supportive if I need him, and encourages me always to make my own decisions and be active in life without him unless I ask for his input. This has helped me to appreciate my husband in so many ways, which adds tons of passion to our relationship since I am authentically grateful for him accepting me as I am.

The ability to be able to learn who I am as a woman is what distinguishes this relationship from my previous one. My likes, my dislikes, my strength and empowerment are all important to my husband. I did not have this opportunity to find who I was until I ended my former relationship at the age of 32. The challenges in this relationship have been centered around staying grounded. Sometimes I become so empowered I have to stop and make sure I am giving the same to him because I know he will always do or say whatever I wish, and do what he can to make sure I am fulfilled. It fills his ego to ensure that I am fulfilled, but I never want him to feel taken for granted. I want him to know he is adored and appreciated.

Even though it has been 10 years since I got out of a Domestic violence relationship, I often cry from what I went through. My husband in this relationship never judges me, he hurts for me. If I need to be alone he gives me space. If I cry he does what he can to meet my needs. He never asks why do I still hurt, or says to get over it. He makes me stronger by reminding me I will never go through that again, that he is here for me and I am worthy of the world. He encourages me to dress sexy, go out with friends, have drinks and go dancing without him, while he watches the kids. He never asks questions or feels jealous, even when I ask him if he ever is. He tells me, all those men can look all they want, but I know who my wife is coming home to. With that encouragement and trust who would ever want to be so silly to not appreciate such a man, a man with so much confidence and passion for his wife? It makes me grateful and so much more in love with him.

My husband is soft spoken, gentle, and super passionate. He listens to me when I speak, never has he raised his voice, but lets me vent. He doesn't mind if I ask him to cook tonight, clean the house or take over the care of the kids. He's a good man with a heart of gold and Thrives on my happiness, and knows I think very highly of him as a person. If more men were like my husband there would be a lot more peace in the world.

I think a lot of women meet these type of men and pass them off as their friend. You need to take your chance with the good guy, the guy you see as a friend. It's important that even though you are that strong independent woman you need to give in a bit and be vulnerable a bit and give to him so it's a two way street. When a good, passionate and encouraging man feels appreciated, he will give you the whole world.

I Don't Have Time to Be His Mom

My FLR relationship with my husband is evolving. I was just on a college campus on a business trip, and noted that Women outnumbered men two-to-one, and the men were subdued. In the wake of the ME TOO movement, men are intimidated and afraid to talk to us until we determine what they can say. That is more power than I need, and more than Women should have, which speaks to how my FLR is evolving.

I am thinking that a healthy marriage can't be as one-sided as I have portrayed, and so far practiced. Although I have always viewed my parents' marriage as healthy with my Mother strictly in charge and requiring my dad's obedience, I now, in my own marriage am increasingly concerned with abuse that demeans or devalues my marriage partner. Women have seen much of this in the past by emotionally-abusive men, and now that things are reversed, I am beginning to think that in a healthy marriage relationship, both partners need the ability to negotiate and compromise, and there has to be a degree of mutual sacrifice - for the welfare of our relationship and mental health of my husband.

I think there may be what someone has called "controlling abuse." I am thinking of when I use my power to prohibit my husband from making any independent decisions, control how he spends his free time, what he wears, what friends he chooses, how much time he spends with friends or family, what and how he thinks.

I am beginning to think that the level of control I am exercising over him may be abusive. We are talking through it together. I am trying to figure out how I may have to change in order for him to be a healthy responsible man/marriage partner, and feel free to assert himself more, and be able to ask me anything and receive an appropriate loving response. We are also working out what degree my power over him is just fetish, and what part he subscribes to because I am superior.

There's no question that I will retain final authority, and final decision-making but I want it to be a relationship where I lead, but he is himself, and is contributing to the relationship in terms of his intelligence, personality, opinions, and where we decide together where he can act or decide independently from my authority.

I certainly believe that we, as Women, need to be in control of our society at all levels. While I prefer to refer to God in the Feminine (because She created both male and Female in Her image and the Female certainly was created with superior traits and capabilities), I have to believe that She values men as well as Women, and it will be unfortunate if we enslave them, or are unloving or disrespectful to them.

My personal dominance of men in my office (professional equals) I believe is a result of being open, friendly, and approachable. When combined with a "dash" of flirtatiousness, it is a recipe for respect and appreciation both ways, but it ends up in the men wanting to please and serve me. Meaning, that I believe I am the opposite of that Woman whom men are afraid to talk to.

I have all the freedoms and power, but I am leading the relationship in such a way that my husband has the freedom to be the man I married, for reasons I married him. He should have his own personality and individuality, and freedom to make decisions, at least within certain parameters.

Granting him these freedoms will help my husband because he will maintain (or in some cases restore) his personality, individuality, and confidence. He will also now be able to make decisions and make choices, again within parameters. Even where the decisions are not available to him, he will have fair input to the decision which will be made by me. Our relationship will benefit because of his confidence level, and because we will both be free to use our strengths to bear on the pre-determined direction(s) of the marriage. Both partners in the relationship have to be happy and fulfilled to make a happy and rewarding, and purposeful marriage.

At first, I thought I would NOT benefit, because I would be giving up some control and scaling back my authority. However, since starting this, he is much happier and more motivated, and I don't have to make EVERY little decision, and the communication we have at new levels and early in looming decisions or processes, that communication is eliminating the possibility and need for absolute obedience on his part. I have discovered that I don't have time to be his Mom, and I prefer to be his dominant Wife.

Make no mistake, I am still the final authority, and he fully supports my leading the relationship and being in control. But we are benefiting from "partnering" in more areas, and admitting that each of us has strengths and weaknesses, which is hard for me to admit of myself, but it is true. It is productive to depend on the other partner where his/her strengths can compensate for weaknesses. Personally, I gain a more competent, happy partner. I gain time to concentrate on our relationship needs and the direction of our marriage and the fulfillment of my mate personally. I gain more time for myself by not having to micromanage everything, make every decision, and police his obedience. I have traded punishment for disobedience, for meaningful communication and unity of purpose and goals, and this, I believe, will improve our relationship dramatically.

He Waited For Me to Initiate Everything

I am from southeast Louisiana, specifically, I lived in a couple small towns about 20 minutes outside New Orleans. I went to a private Catholic school from pre-K to 8th grade. My parents divorced shortly before high school, then switched to public school. My senior year of high school is when Hurricane Katrina hit. Luckily, we didn't personally have any major damage, but I was out of school for 2 weeks, my brother was unable to return to Loyola University for an entire semester, so he dropped out for a while.

Katrina was the event that made me decide to not seek a job after college anywhere south of I-10 and I-12. Which is why I ended up working in rural central Louisiana after grad school. I have a bachelors in psychology and a masters in counseling, specifically school counseling. I moved 3 hours away from home to central Louisiana simply for the job, so I knew no one, and I'm not the type to mingle at bars or randomly strike up conversation with a cute stranger. So I joined Match.com after my 3-year relationship ended (due to my ex's addiction problems primarily along with a drug-induced manic episode that got ugly). Match is where I met my husband Eric. He is from Houston, and like me, he moved to central Louisiana after college for work; he's an interpretive ranger at a state park.

The relationship with my ex is where I began building my confidence. He was a man so preoccupied with feeling like he had to portray qualities of manliness. As a result, he suffered with self-esteem issues and felt inadequate whenever I paid for things, which for most of the relationship even while struggling through full-time grad school while also working full-time retail. I paid for everything. He struggled holding jobs. I paid our rent and utilities and food. I would say that this financial independence while in a relationship helped to build my confidence in myself to not establish dependence on a man to take care of me. This relationship also made me realize that, at minimum, I wanted my next relationship to be equal, to be mutual in everything, because I was so tired of feeling like I was expected to do everything. For example, the ex and I would argue about doing dishes/cleaning, mostly during one of the times where he was unemployed. I would come home to mess that for the sake of not arguing, I would clean.

I wanted a more 50/50 relationship where I didn't have to compromise and sacrifice so much on my end, where it felt like it was my sole responsibility to make and keep us both happy. And a lot of that ties into my desire to have someone treat me the way I treat him. Even when "arguing", since I make a point of not yelling or name-calling or belittling when I get upset, I'd appreciate the same effort from my partner.

I made a point of emphasizing some of this in my Match profile. I went on a couple dates before I met Eric, and while they were nice enough, I didn't feel that connection. Right off the bat, Eric was different. He wanted to be led, even before he and I realized that's what I was meant to do. On our first date, I did most of the talking, which was unusual to me since I was used to a guy trying to talk himself up to impress me. On the second date, I offered to pay for it, even making a comment about how I don't want to insult him or feel like I was taking away his "man-card" by offering. He had no problem, nor was he insulted, that he was actually thankful. Prior to this date, we talked about our salaries, and discovered I made more by about $10k, so me being the realist I am, I thought it unfair to expect him to always pay for our dates.

As our relationship became official and progressed, I noticed how much of a gentleman he was, yet at the same time, waited for me to initiate everything. I'm the one who initially messaged him on Match. I was the one to ask him to be my boyfriend. I was the first to hold his hand. I was the first to kiss him. I was the first to initiate foreplay and sex with him. He was the first to say, "I love you."

Admittedly, it wasn't easy to initiate much of that because I was so used to a man showing the initial interest, and playing pursuer. At one point blatantly I had to ask him if he saw me as more than a friend because he didn't do all those "firsts." He was difficult to read, but I'm not afraid to be open and honest about my perceptions, assumptions, thoughts, and feelings, so once we had that conversation, it went a lot smoother. During the conversation, he literally said that it was because he respected me so much, that he never wanted to feel like he was taking a step that I wasn't ready for, so he waited for me to lead. Six months after our first date we were engaged. A year and a half later, we were married.

Since getting married, we started off great and continue to do great especially after Eric came up with the "contract". It basically outlines our roles and expectations in our household, which has helped tremendously to avoid any conflict. Eric is the type to enjoy getting things done; he has various to-do lists and budget sheets to keep track of everything, and then enjoys doing everything on the lists. Eric does about 95% of the cleaning and 99% of the cooking in large part due to me focusing on my career, which often means staying late to get things done. He enjoys that I am the breadwinner, and it makes him feel good that he does so much around the house to help make me happy. Of course, I help him when I can as I would hate myself if I ever felt like I was taking him for granted. He has told me many times that my happiness makes him happy, so he does all he can to ensure it, which is why he doesn't mind cooking because he knows I don't particularly enjoy doing it. Currently, it is just us two. We plan to have children in about two years but there's more hiking we want to do before we get kinda bogged down with child rearing for a while.

After we completed our contract and realized that we really do have a very non-traditional relationship. It was more matriarchal, as I make all important decisions in our relationship and Eric consults me before spending any money, for example. Eric actually did research and eventually found your website and shared it with me. It was hard to find a name to give our relationship because obviously most that comes up was femdom (which we have elements of that in our sexual life, but I don't seek to constantly humiliate or ever disrespect or belittle him). It was almost like a breath of fresh air, a kind of realization or "coming out" when we found your website! I think it was the article about the two types of FLRs that he found first because it went into the Loving FLR, which described us to a T!

Currently, no one knows how extensive our relationship is in this regard. I have made comments to coworkers before about my husband doing all the cooking and they have given me funny looks. I don't bring it up further than that at work because of the very traditional views of the culture out here; it's very religious. I have heard the local preacher preach those quotes from the Bible about the woman being subservient to the man so there's a lot of that mentality where the woman's place is in the kitchen and tending to children, and that men just don't do that. Because of this, I avoid telling people that live around here the details of our relationship just to not have to deal with the awkwardness that comes from people who aren't known to be open to non-traditional things.

My mom is the only one to which I've mentioned how my relationship works, with how my husband takes care of everything in order to make me happy. Currently, discovering the official name for our relationship dynamic is refreshing, but I am still working on my overall confidence in leading this much. My husband has his part down for sure, but I am still not used to having someone be ok with me making all the decisions in a relationship!

I Am Clearly the Leader and Boss

I grew up in a home where Mom was boss, females were superior, and men, though loved, respected, and cared for, were respectful and obedient to the Women/Girls. My brother and Father had to obey my Mom. When I reached age 14, I became "the Woman of the house," when Mom was gone, and my brother and Dad had to obey me.

Today, my father, brother and I have a great relationship. They don't resent me in any way, even though they continue to be respectful to me. I think it's because my Mother modeled and taught me, and I continue to love and respect men, and want the best for them. I don't believe in putting them down, or hurting them or being sadistic towards them. They are inferior in abilities and roles, but they are equal in God's sight.

They are simple, but wonderful when loved, respected and cared for. When I was in my upper teens, I was vested with disciplinary authority if they disobeyed, but even through that, I always treated them (and all men) with respect and admiration. We were a loving and highly-functioning family, and remain loving, caring, and respectful to each other.

I have never had a relationship that was not a FLR. I have dominated boys since I was little, and dominated them in high school and college. As I mentioned, I am not a feminist (the way they are currently understood in culture), but I believe in Female Superiority, and I guess I would have to classify myself as a Female Supremacist.

I recently turned 26 and my husband recently turned 27. I met my husband at church. I am 5'10" and 135 lbs and he is 5'11", so in heels I tower over him. I have large feet so I can easily wear 4" or 5" heels, making me 6'3". Since I am also approachable, confident, and friendly, men notice me. He attracted me because he was fit, intelligent, personable, and humble.

I am clearly the leader and boss. While I consider his input and ideas, my decisions are final and unquestioned. You may think this extreme, but my husband took my name(s) in marriage, and freely admits that the relationship depends on my leadership, and obeys me. I love, honor and respect him, his abilities, etc. but I am NOT a feminist. I love men, respect men, and want men to achieve to their highest potential. I just believe what Women have always known, and as empirical data now shows, that Women are Superior to men. We are smarter, better at relationships, more articulate, better managers, better problem-solvers and better decision-makers.

In the early dating times, this became obvious in our dating relationship. Although he is confident and professional (commercial pilot), I am stronger and more dominant, and he realized over time that I was better at leading, including decisions and relationships. So when we started becoming more serious, we had these "superiority" discussions, and he agreed that Women are superior in general, and in most ways that count in life and culture, and he willingly submitted to my leadership.

In his words . . . *"I believe you are better qualified to lead us, and I want to surrender to your authority, submit to your leadership and decisions, and obey you."* Yes of course, I, over time, led him in those words. I also control his sexual desires (keep him at whatever sexual temperature is required to reinforce his desire to focus on me and please me), and any/all of his sexual releases.

We have been together two years, and married this past September (I am not proud that I consented to "be together" before we were married - I don't believe in premarital sex or co-habitation). Our relationship works well. I respect him, love him and take care of him. He loves me and obeys me, and desires to please me. Even though he is a commercial pilot, I out-earn him, and can support us, so he has reduced his employment to part-time (his flies for a corporation), so he can keep up more "domestic" duties, and please his wife.

In my home, my husband has to obey me, and I have been known to punish him for disobedience. But our relationship is pretty well-established, so this is very rare. Even though I am the boss, I do receive his input/suggestions about most things, before making my decision. But when made, my decisions are not contested in any way. I am pretty dominant.

He Never Says No To Me

I t is hard to find good information on Female Led Relationships online. Most websites show so many photos about men being treated like animals and women being so mean. Our FLR does not have any of that. Our FLR does not have kink at all.

My friend Casey told me about FLRs when a man she met online asked her if she knew about them. During her research she found so many websites about orgasm control and punishments that she was turned off and stopped speaking to him. I started doing my own online research and saw the same thing until I read something about Loving FLRs and it linked to this site. As I read the stories and advice I was excited. I told Casey about Loving FLR and we both agreed that it made sense. Not only did it make sense, I think I already have a Loving FLR with my husband and he doesn't know it.

My husband and I have created our dream lives together. He's a teacher. I am a business consultant. We live just outside of Montreal. I am 36 and he is 53. We met at a mutual friend's birthday party and I thought he was kind when he offered me a ride home afterwards and did not make a move on me. He was patient with me as I disentangled myself from a messy divorce during that time. We were friends first but I saw traits that my ex-husband didn't have. Sometimes I think I married my ex-husband just so that I would learn what to avoid in a real loving relationship.

We have been married for 2 years now and I have no complaints. He makes sure of that. He does a lot for me. He likes the little Gentleman type things like massages and telling me how beautiful I am every day. We pay bills together, but he pays more even though I earn more than he does. I don't have total control over him. I don't have to control his orgasms. I don't keep tabs on where he is. He doesn't have to ask me for permission for anything. He is his own man and that is what I like most about him.

He makes great decisions when he has to. Most of the time we take turns to decide what we want to eat and other decisions like where to vacation. He never makes me feel sad. He never argues with me when it's really important to me. We hang out together more than we do with our other friends but we have separate social lives where I go out with Casey and other ladies from my networking groups when I can.

I pamper him just as much as he pampers me. I love cooking for him, running errands for him if he is tired and sometimes I give him massages. I enjoy doing those things for him and he always says he appreciates it.

The reason I believe I have a Loving FLR is when we have a big decision to make, I always have the final say. I don't have to fight for it. I never have to argue. He will say what he has to say and then ask me what I want. When I tell him what I want he will think about it for a second and then he gives in. Sometimes I will sit there with a smirk on my face because I know he's just pretending to consider my choice. He never says No to me.

I have never been much of a leader. I am a go with the flow type of woman. In my group of friends there are other women who are more bossy and try to take charge all of the time. I'm pretty relaxed with everyone. With him I don't feel like I'm leading but from what I have read about Loving FLRs I am. I am leading when it comes to the things that are important to me. When I don't know what I want or what we should do, we talk it out, he presents options for me to make it easier for me to choose and then I choose. He goes along with whatever I decide.

It seems like having a Loving FLR is about the man's decision to give the woman what she wants. If you have a partner who wants to argue or fight with you and doesn't want to listen to you when you tell him that something is important to you then that's not a Loving FLR. A Loving FLR, at least in my home, is when your partner wants you to be happy and does what he can to make sure that you are. My husband is like that. I didn't have to train him or write out a contract or punish him. That's who he is and I am so glad I found him.

Our Loving FLR Helped My Wife Tremendously

My wife and I live an older neighborhood of well-manicured houses. The setting is private and we like it that way. My lovely wife and I spend a lot of time traveling and love road trips. My wife is the bread winner of the family and I take care of the house.

I asked my wife if she had ever heard of FLR. What did she say? She was not sure, not unhappy but confused. She was not sure why someone would like to be hurt. She was thinking of some leather clad dominatrix.

I had laid my cards on the table, I had to continue. I explained it was not like that and I wanted her to feel special, that I would do anything for her. I suggested we start small and that went well, she warmed up to me helping around the house and cooking. When did she really take full control? When I lost my job. I had more time and no reason not to take care of all domestic tasks. I started getting dinner ready by the time she got home and having a glass of wine ready for her. But I think it was the foot messages that she really enjoyed. She started asking and googling about FLR then.

The biggest thing that has changed because of our FLR is the relationship with my wife. We were good before but we are better now. I have such a deeper understanding of her now. We have a lot of very intimate moments and that brings out a lot of sharing. Not necessarily sexual moments but things like washing and drying her hair, shaving her legs, painting her nails and pampering. We talk and joke during these times, very personal times.

As far as the biggest benefit- the easing of frustrations. We have a regulated routine and find we have less ego and more time. The challenges are becoming set in our ways and the feeling of not being listened to (that's my issue).

My wife is a very smart person but growing up she was always put down. Our Loving FLR helped my wife tremendously. First was the knowledge that someone was in her corner and second she realized she could be assertive. This is a good thing when someone has always felt hushed by authority figures.

I am a man who likes be behind the scenes. I think my wife has taken a liking to the spotlight. Much like of an ugly duckling story, she feels she has blossomed into a beautiful swan which totally works for me.

I make it seem as though it happened quickly but establishing our Loving FLR took a couple of years. First was the total rejection of her idea that this relationship was about hurting me. I proved to her that that was not the point. Communication and going slow are the way to go. I was hurt when I laid myself out and expressed what I wanted. I felt rejected when I did not happen right away. My advice to couples hoping to establish a Loving FLR is to keep an open mind and don't shut down ideas. Listen to what she really wants, you may come to like the explanation.

Being Introduced to Loving FLRs has Been Refreshing

I am at a point in my life where I can almost exhale. My career has served me well with travel both in and out of the U.S. Now I am mentoring others and looking forward to leaving the 9 to 5 grind of healthcare compliance reimbursement. The next phase of my life involves more creative endeavors and volunteer work with several non-profits that focus on hunger and making learning easier for all people.

I grew up in a very, very small town in Alabama and found escape through books. I realized early in life that there was so much to explore and to see in this world. I placed my wanderlust on hold, got married and settled into the routine of life. Was it a FLR? No it was not. But as I reflect on those 14 years, I can see where I was more of the leader. It was considered being "bossy." I did want and expect things done in a certain way...my way. The women on my mother's side of the family were all strong, in charge types and men seemed to be quiet followers. After the divorce, my focus was on raising my child. At age 53, the idea of exploring the world is still alive. Now that my child has finished college and started her career, I travel yearly with a group of female friends. I know travel would be more enjoyable with a gentleman that will embrace me, my dreams and enjoy sharing in the new phase of my life......all within a loving FLR.

I spent time reflecting on past relationships. The one thing that stood out was that I was the one directing the relationships. So I started to research the dynamic of what I thought was a bossy woman. The picture or definition I saw for a woman in charge of her man did not define me and was not what I wanted. So I kept researching and discovered FLRs and immediately connected with what I found. It was refreshing to see that it was "okay" to be a woman in charge of her man/relationship in a loving and real way. It was such a relief to find that there are men who also want this who are normal....they work, have interests, friends and are successful.

Being introduced to Loving FLRs has been a wonderful and refreshing boost to my search for a relationship. I completely accept who I am in terms of what I need and seek in a relationship. The idea of being in a loving FLR makes me smile inside!

The happiness, emotional well-being, personal satisfaction and realization of dreams for the woman in a FLR is a huge benefit of being in a loving FLR. When this happens, the man and children (if any) benefit from the female's loving and wise guidance, this becoming the best they can be also. Some couples may be challenged by what other people think about their relationship and feel pressure to conform to the norm of other opinions. I believe that what happens in a loving relationship is between the two involved and if the bond is solid can withstand outside challenges. The only challenge I encountered was in finding a partner. But of course all challenges can be overcome!

I have recently started a relationship with my new gentleman who was raised in a strict, loving matriarchal home. Seeing a woman in charge of her man and a man who happily surrendered to his wife's direction was what he saw/experienced as a child.

My new gentleman and I were having dinner for our first date. We were at a great restaurant and the ambiance was perfect. The waiter came over and I ordered for him...from wine and appetizer to the entrée. My man did not complain or refuse any of my choices. The waiter's reaction was priceless! He was a little taken aback. It was apparent that he had not seen a couple where the woman was in charge. I totally enjoyed the moment!

My gentleman fully embraces FLRs. Our interactions have been very effortless because we both know we work better in a FLR. We can freely discuss FLR dynamics and other topics from politics to books and art. He is very smart, caring and most of all, a complete gentleman who shares my passion for learning and traveling. We are both excited about the journey that has started!

To learn more about FLRs any woman or man should look to the Internet. There are so many sites out there that address FLRs and are in English, German and other languages. The site lovingflr.com helped to answer my questions and provided a tool to learn more. Many good books are also available from the website and bookstores. My best advice......read, read and read some more. Befriend others who want or are already in FLRs for support and social outlets. I believe that if I had been introduced to FLRs in my 20s, I would have made different choices and would be in a Loving FLR marriage. Remember that your FLR reflects who you are as individuals and how you come together as a couple. It won't be a carbon copy of anything you read or encounter.

It is great that more women are becoming empowered to embrace leadership roles in their relationships. We can be strong, confident, loving AND in charge in our relationships!

She Makes Policy and I Work Out the Details

Hi! I am Erik. In daily life I work as director of an investment management firm (co-owned by myself). My work is not my hobby, but it comes close especially during periods in which markets are good. But the real hobbies - independent of markets, are chess, swimming, music (playing the piano), and doing nice things with my girlfriend Mudiwa. These nice things can range from going out for dinner, a party, seeing a movie, attending a wine tasting to short-stay city trips and longer holidays. We both love travel. Both I and Mudiwa are pretty close with our respective families, but they all live relatively far away from each other. When look at 'us', our own family consists at the moment of just her and me. But we won't rule out adding newcomers soon, but only after marriage!

I myself knew that I like a certain power imbalance in relationships. But although I checked out the BDSM world online, it was immediately clear that it was not ME. But it wasn't until I met Mudiwa that I knew what was happening and what it was that I was looking for, a Female Led Relationship. Together we discovered this, with Mudiwa knowing more than I did. I had the feeling that this was finally a relationship in which I could be ME, as opposed to playing a kind of role.

The biggest benefit for us has been that the power balance is a natural one, as a result of which we truly operate as a TEAM. We did not really have big challenges as far as interaction with each other is concerned. The challenge is most likely the reactions of outsiders (friends, family) who will one or the other way assume that it is freaky, kinky or even worse: BDSM. Our task therefore to show that we are happy and that this works for us, without signs of being freaky! I am proud that I did not just 'define' things for myself (together with Mudiwa), but that I am also willing to tell people that I am in a Female Led Relationship.

I think that in our case the perfect fit is the result of a Love-based power imbalance in which Mudiwa leads most of the time but not in a template-like manner. We go from case to case and topic to topic. Based on our expertise we will then more or less automatically decide who will lead. We sometimes joke saying that if Mudiwa is the Queen or Princess in her Kingdom, that I am then the Prime Minister. She makes policy and I work out details. She reigns and I support and serve.

Now it is a matter of being firm, explaining to others why this works for us and not just that: why it is not so weird. If let's say 2 out of 3 men are natural dominants and 1 out of 3 women are natural dominants, then a true natural FLR couple is a relationship type that works best for 1/3 times. 1/3 = 11 percent of the people. And that is still a huge group in society.

In previous, non-FLR relationships I did often struggle with communication and lack of clarity. With Mudiwa all this is much easier. At home we have clear rules and I try to adhere to them as much as I can. And not just that, I show my dedication in a pro-active manner. One of the things Mudiwa and I enjoy most is when she allows me to be her personal assistant when dressing up. I find it a relaxing time together when helping her with her clothes, nails, makeup and hair. My family has a fashion background and it is nice to see that Mudiwa appreciates my feedback and suggestions. Whenever my contribution (style suggestions or hands-on support tasks) was good, she shows me her appreciation with compliments and tokens of affection. It makes me very happy; a kind of happiness that I did not know to this extent in most of my other relationships earlier in life.

The nice thing is that by being so actively involved with Mudiwa's styling, she also provided me with sufficient knowledge about what she likes in this respect. Result: whenever I see nice things for her in the mall or at a specialized store, it is relatively easy for me to translate this into a surprise token of dedication. Obviously I know the sizes she wears.

It may sound weird but for me the biggest gain when comparing FLR with ordinary relationships is in its clarity. Of course, like in any love-based relationship between two people there will always be little misunderstandings and conflicts. But in FLR these can be dealt with in a clear and straightforward manner. The clear distribution of tasks in the relationship helps as well. It is therefore hardly ever that we have issues that last longer than a few hours, with each one of us understanding the other very well. Since our relationship is based on love with a big capital L, we both try to be fair and judge the behavior of the other based on the clear rules and distribution of tasks set out in the beginning. Whenever things do lead to little tensions along the way, we can easily incorporate them in an update of the rules or distribution of tasks. This way the structure of our FLR relationship is capable of strengthening our love even further.

Does that mean that in FLR nothing could lead to a bigger conflict? No, that would not be realistic. But when it is more severe, we do know exactly how to solve it. After all Mudiwa is in charge. I find it much easier to show dedication and love in such a clear-cut setting than in one guided by far more complicated communication (or lack thereof) in earlier relationships.

We Play the Roles We Really Want to Play

I am a college professor who lives in Madison, Wisconsin and just turned 52. I have been married for 24 years with my loving and devoted husband. We have two kids, who have both gone off to college and other places. We miss them, but we're taking advantage of our time alone and enjoying more theater and live music, including weekend trips to bigger cities. I love to travel, and my work has taken me all over the world.

My husband and I met and fell in love in graduate school. We could see that other academic couples had a hard time finding jobs in the same city, unless one person, usually the woman, was less ambitious. He told me that if I wanted a tenure-track job, he'd go wherever I got one. He'd be happy working as an adjunct and playing the supporting role for my career. I believed him, because he loved to cook and do housework. He even likes grocery shopping, which I can't stand. We hadn't heard the term FLR, but that's what we've had from early on. When the kids came along, we shared the work pretty equally. During the pregnancy (of course) and first months I did more and took some time off, but afterward he was the one with more flexible schedule.

I've never felt constrained in my career. I can work late, travel, and pretty much do what I want, knowing that my husband is doing what he wants. His teaching is fulfilling for him, but his real calling in life is doing whatever I need him to do. I would have been willing to share the cooking and housework, but I'm happy to let him take care of all that. I do manage our finances, partly because I'm better at doing it, but also because I like being on top of them. As for decision making, we decide all important financial and parenting matters together, but in other areas, when we disagree, I know I can have the last word if I want to. I don't "pull rank" very often, but I appreciate knowing that I can. When I do, my husband is disappointed at first, but that disappointment quickly fades, and he loves seeing me assert myself in this way. He won't pretend to prefer ballroom dancing to football, but if I put my foot down, he'll not only be happier watching the dancing with me, he'll ask me if he can rub that foot.

The best thing is that both my husband and I are able to play the roles that we really want to play. The challenge is dealing with societal expectations, and especially the expectations of some of our extended family. The fact that I didn't change my name when I got married is somehow noteworthy. My husband wishes that he had taken my last name, but he just couldn't bring himself to do it.

Last month, my colleague was visiting from London. She was giving a talk in my department. She is a friend I've collaborated with over the years, but she'd never met my husband. When she came over for dinner, she was blown away by how he prepared everything so beautifully. We had a great time from the hors d'oeuvres on the deck to the after-dinner drinks in the living room. My husband was charming and attentive without being subservient. There was something so natural about how he handled everything and let us enjoy our time together. My friend's partner, a woman, also plays a supporting role for her and her career. Now that we are all empty nesters, we want to get them together.

He's secure of his masculinity, a strong and tough guy who enjoys chopping wood one minute and ironing my blouses the next. For a man, he is not a bad listener, and he's never envious of my success or my opportunities to do things like travel to so many places. He enjoys my trips vicariously and wants to hear all about them, and he loves to be the one that I can always count on. He'd do anything for me.

For women, I'd say that if you really want to pursue your career and have a sane family life, there are definitely men who would love the chance to switch the traditional roles. They don't have to be house husbands. They can work. They just can't be in careers that are too demanding of their time. For many men, there is nothing sexier than a confident and assertive woman.

You can let your man tell you about his fantasies, but that doesn't mean he should expect you to fulfill them. I'm not much for role play anyway, but knowing a few of my husband's fantasies gives me insight into him, and it is a way for him to open up to me and be a little vulnerable. That in itself is exciting for him. But if his fantasies enter a realm that you are uncomfortable with, you need to let him know that there are certain things he needs to keep to himself.

He Shows Me His Love & Devotion Daily

We are kind of retired from the tech field. We developed some programs we have sold, some we maintain but nowhere near full-time. We hang out at home, fish, camp and enjoy the outdoors. We have some acreage with a couple of horses and a comfortable home just outside the city. We enjoy traveling and seeing new things. My hubby proposed the FLR lifestyle. I researched it, we discussed it and here we are. It seemed like a win/win for me...so we went with it.

We both enjoy the opportunities it provides. It's been most beneficial to me and made us stronger as a couple. At the same time I've experienced freedoms and liberties I would never have even considered before. I'm extremely happy to be in a Loving Female Led Relationship. I'm constantly spoiled and always try and return comfort to my hubby. We are more in tune with each other's needs and wants. I needed to develop a much stronger persona...which I did and I love it. But it was difficult at first, a complete role change in our dynamic.

I constantly hear how attentive and caring my husband is and how others wish they had that. I think it's all about communication and we've developed a whole new level. Thomas shows me his love and devotion daily as well as feelings he couldn't or didn't share so openly before. We went through a period of trial and error for some time. At times his attention level and attentiveness was just too much, borderline annoying. He worked a lot on when and how to touch me, paying closer attention to my moods and understanding my needs.

We now have a daily routine we follow most mornings and evenings, talking about what we're doing each day, spelling out what we need to accomplish. Some days we have no goals and he is typically charged with presenting some activity scenarios. He usually plans our date nights. He has no problem including anything I suggest or altering his plan. Often date night is a movie at home and snuggling, just enjoying us. We no longer go through the - What do you want to do today...I don't know, how about you? - scenario. He usually knows exactly what I want or creates some new and interesting things to do that he thinks I might enjoy.

Thomas and I have developed patterns so he knows when I'm in my office I don't need him to be there. Certain areas of the home we respect each other's privacy and do our own thing. Each day we work to accomplish what we've discussed that morning, knowing we can share the rest of the day and evening as a couple. Some days he needs to get away and do some things he wants, and I try to allow that time for him. I have certain nights, times I go out alone or with my friends to shop, have a drink or whatever. He still has a monthly poker night with the boys and usually has some time to pursue his other hobbies.

My most rewarding experience came last year with my mother in law. I was not always her favorite person, but we've gotten closer over the years. Thomas has a rather large extended family. At last year's family reunion my mother in law commented that it was obvious that her son and I had a deep and lasting love. She was always worried he would become introverted and anti-social. With me he seems to have a confidence and passion that spreads to everyone. Thomas shows traits her husband never could and she seemed somewhat jealous. The way he looks at me, holds me, interacts with me shows we have a true partnership and are in tune with one another. In short she said that we were good for each other and whatever we were doing was working well.

His sister mentioned that he was so much more focused. She always thought he could have A.D.D. Now he is a great listener and conversationalist. Her brother and dad never gave hugs or showed much emotion, but he does now. She agreed that we make a great team/couple. A Loving Female Led Relationship was something my husband wanted, and now we both do.

My Biggest Goal is to Never Tell Her No

I purchased your book, *She Wants*, for my wife almost half a year ago now, and she read it cover to cover without hardly putting it down. We discovered that she is a classic Goddess! She loves getting service, devotion, and pampering. She loves being adored and knowing that I focus all of my time and attention on her. She does not demand it, and she knows that I gladly provide it out of love and desire. She in no way has to nag, threaten or coerce me to have my attention and devotion.

My wife had an epiphany as a result of your website and your book. She told me that she has always desired love in the ways I give it to her, but, prior to this epiphany, she always thought she was being too selfish and demanding for having those desires. I started by giving her the attention and devotion before she even knew what I was up to. I firmly believe that the most effective way to lead your wife or girlfriend into a Loving FLR is by quietly showing her the benefits. I was, and still am, always certain to open every door for her, assist her with her coat, carry any packages or bags for her (including her purse at times,) walk beside or just a step behind her, drop her off at the door, keep an umbrella over her in the rain, serve dinner to her and jump at the chance to refresh her drink. I try to anticipate her needs with the goal of her never even having to ask for what she desires. This is the life I have dreamed of for as long as I can remember.

My earliest memories of wanting to serve a woman were at age five, and I tell her often that she has made my five-year-old dreams come true! Even though I told her often that I loved serving, pampering, and adoring her she was still skeptical, and she still felt guilt over allowing me to do it. She very much enjoyed it, but she still felt that shouldn't and couldn't desire to be loved like that. It was your site, LovingFLR.com and your book that showed her that she was not the only woman that desired love in that way, that I was not the only man that desired to give love in that way, and that she was not alone. Not only was she not alone, but there was an entire community out there that shared our desires. She no longer felt alone or different.

I have had these desires my entire life, and I count myself lucky that I feel comfortable sharing them with the woman I love and trust. I know that there are many men out there that truly love their wives yet feel that they cannot share their true feelings and desires. My wife too had to be led into her rightful place in our Loving FLR. She thought that she wasn't allowed to have love in the way she desired it.

It hit me that desiring a Loving FLR might be equated to being homosexual two to three decades ago. Homosexuality has only become acceptable (if you can call it that) in the mainstream within the last decade.

Prior to that there was not much info made publicly available about it, and a lot of homosexual individuals had feelings very much like my wife had. They felt that they could not and should not desire to be loved that way. They felt like they were the only one out there that had those desires, and that no one else could possibly understand. I think that much of human sexuality is that way really. Regardless of one's desires it is a taboo subject.

I think one of the first ways to help people feel good about making their Loving FLR public is to let them know that they are not alone, and that it is ok to desire to give or receive love in that way. You are doing a wonderful job of starting that off. Both myself and my wife are glad to let others see our Loving FLR in action. It's the, "actions speak louder than words" concept. I am quite proud to let others see me open every door for her, go to any length to meet her smallest need, and carry her purse and packages while she shops. That does not stem from any desire on my part to be publicly humiliated. That is not a desire I have, and my wife would hate it! It stems from the fact that I do love and adore her tremendously, and I am proud for others to see that. I do not change my actions in public or around family; I just simply refer to her as ma'am instead of Goddess.

My wife has no interest in femdom, hurting me or humiliating me, and that works very well for us. Ours is a Goddess and knight relationship that centers on my complete loving devotion to her and attention to her needs and wishes. I have told her many times that one of my biggest goals is to never tell her no.

She Was In Charge of the Family

My name is Max and I live in England. I was in a long female led relationship 30 years ago. It was a loving one and I cannot say we ever had an argument. It was nice. This was what my wife wanted from the start and I was very unsure at first but soon got used to it.

I was in the British army and went away a lot and we had children so I did not need any money at all when I was away on service. All my pay went into my wife's bank always so she could run the home and when I came home she was in charge of the home and family and what she said was final.

In the military I lived in a man's world; kill or be killed. I was so happy to step out of the man's world and into a female led world because I could let go of daily stress of life in the army. I am in no way soft and I am very manly and very fit at age 59. My wife paid the bills and made all the decisions in life, I just followed her and had no problems with that. At home I was father and house husband. I would cook and my wife sat back and I loved to follow her lead. This was not a kink or a fetish, this was what I wanted to do and the way I wanted to live my life and I was so happy to leave the man's world behind me.

My wife did cheat on me and I walked out. She had this idea that in a FLR a wife could have a part time lover but

I look at it like this; in a male led relationship it is wrong for the man to cheat on the woman so I should have the same respect. I loved my wife deeply and it was the worst thing that could happen to me.

I still remember the good times though. I loved to take her a cup of tea and sit talking about what we were going to do that day. She always made plans for us that were exciting and new. She chose my clothes and what she liked me to wear was final. I understand that she had to look at me and I didn't care. She expected me to step up to her standards which I did. If she was happy then I felt good.

To be honest I am on my own now. I have tried to find a new lady but I find in England the ladies don't understand a loving female led relationship. They seem to think it's a kink and I can tell you this is no kink, it's for real. I do not like whips, chains, leather or femdom. I feel robbed that society in the UK is still back in the Victorian period concerning relationships. This is so annoying to me. I want women to stand up take charge and stop following a program you have had put into your head that men are supposed to be the dominant partner. If this is what you want well, that's ok but, please girls don't let life pass you by. You could be the boss in your own home and have a man who is happy to follow you and be your true lover who places you first.

In England I cannot find a partner who wants to lead. Maybe it is because I have a very broad Lancashire mixed Yorkshire accent and to many posh British this is no good.

I just hope all you ladies who want to lead take the first step and go for it you will be so happy. You will understand true love for the first time. You must understand that female led relationships are not a kink or a fetish. A FLR is a loving modern way of life that is full of rewards for both partners in different ways and the end result is true love. I really do miss this lifestyle but maybe one day I will find a lady who is like minded.

If you're on your first loving female led journey I wish you all the luck in the world. Don't hold back, go for it! Life is yours to enjoy. Love is free. Good luck.

Being the Leader in Your Family Is Possible

Hello Goddesses and Gentlemen. I am a retired Naval officer and Afghan War veteran in my mid 30's. I live on the Virginia coast but I grew up in Kenya with my missionary parents. I have degrees in Islamic Studies and Environmental Health. Since I've been married, though, I have been a homemaker and the primary caregiver of my 8-year-old stepdaughter. I really enjoy sports and spending time outside and at the beach. I also love making crafts, art and sometimes clothes. Besides my stepdaughter, we also sometimes do short term foster care and have at most two other children in the house.

Well I've always been tall for a woman (6'3) so for a long time I've been associated with being strong, confident and dominant - for lack of a better word. I guess I owned that perception and made it my own. So the FLR dynamic felt like a good fit. My husband lost his first wife from an overdose six years ago. When I started dating him and he eventually let me more into his life I saw that this was a family that desperately needs a woman's touch. So once I took charge and brought some organization and order into their lives, he was much happier and very grateful. So when he asked me to marry him and move in, he also asked if I would be head of the house and be the leader. I was so honored and touched. Now I spend my days making schedules, assigning tasks, managing finances and creating a nurturing space for my family.

The way we are living out our FLR is very liberating to me. I started to feel more and more myself. That has been the biggest surprise so far actually.

Even though the concept of a FLR felt natural for me, in other ways it didn't as well. Growing up in my family, there was no question that the leader was my father. And that always worked well. So dealing with those conflicting thoughts were challenging at first.

A more long term challenge is knowing which leadership style to use. Some situations require me to channel my Navy days and be very assertive and direct, while other situations call for me to be more nurturing and encouraging.

My husband is very resourceful and has had quite a bit of success at his job. Adding my money saving skills to that has been the key for me to be able to be a homemaker. He is also modest and humble. His willingness to be vulnerable and knowing he needed help with running a home made it very easy and natural for me to step in and lead.

One thing I have noticed is that my husband can get burned out. Working full time and family life easily tires him out. Being as selfless as he is, he often forgets to take care of himself. He won't treat himself to the things that he loves like fishing and watching sports and going to the gym. So I learned that I need to add self-care to our schedules. We each get a "Sabbath Day." Mine is Saturday and his is Sunday. This really gives us - especially him - more energy.

My stepdaughter really looks up to me and we've always had a great relationship. She has no reservations about calling me mom or mommy, and I'm finally more comfortable with that now. Now that she's growing up and more aware of relationships and seeing other families, she's very proud that I'm the leader or "the boss" as she says. She has even said to me that she wants my role in family of her own one day. It's very touching and rewarding to know that I could be such a good example for her and for her to know that being a leader is possible for her.

One time we were visiting some neighbors and the subject came up of making a "man cave" in the house. My husband said there's a room in our house where that would work perfectly and my stepdaughter - bless her heart - said "Um... You're gonna have to run that by Mom." Instant laughter all around. This was a cute comment but that was affirming for me to know that she knew what I am and the role that I play in the family.

Jesus Said Love Your Wife as I Love the Church

Who would have thought I would be living in Florida and enjoying a good, fulfilling life at the age of 53. Landscaping is a career I chose for the past 16 years after a career in business that lasted more than 13 years came to a close in early 2001. The choice to landscape freed up my time to realign what is most important in a good and fruitful life. This career change led to a life focusing on my wife and her vision for our family.

Our family is pretty close and we all respect each other and the lives we lead. Our family values are rooted in a strong belief in Jesus as our Lord and Savior. We are not fanatics, but we realize there is a creator and a loving God which loves us. He sacrificed his life for us. By Jesus and His example we love and sacrifice with love for us and others. This is a great way to live. We live to share in an awesome life and go above and beyond to show love. We are empty nesters and enjoy the benefits of living a love filled life raising our family, living and learning each day, one day at a time. We love holidays , sports, garage sales, watching Netflix, participating in our church, going out to dinner, shopping, BBQ's, watching Fox news, reading, singing in the choir, volunteering in community, traveling to see family, and of course social media. Our life is so rewarding doing something for others in our life out of love and commitment to trying to be centered on the lessons Jesus taught.

My whole life manners and respect were taught in our family, school, church and community involvement. My father always respected my mother, based on the respect Jesus gave to His Mother Mary. My wife loves being respected, loved, cherished and being important in our lives. The life is so rewarding for her and our family because of selfless love taught to us by Jesus.

The ability to show your wife love and respect is the most rewarding action a man can do in life. The choice to love and cherish my wife is a reflection of what Jesus taught to man. Jesus said love your wife as I love the church. Selfish people don't see this they only focus on themselves. Living a life full of life and joy is awesome. We must learn to put others, especially the wife, before ourselves. This simple rule builds a life that generations of your family can build off on and into the generations to come.

The biggest benefit of loving your wife is a satisfaction of self-worth and self-respect. It allows us to focus not on the self-interest of ourselves but on the focus of us as a couple. This focus on our lives will lead us through Jesus into eternal life in paradise with Jesus. The biggest challenge for me is to not get lost in lust and stay focused on love. The benefits of loving your wife is fulfilled in ways that send us to the moon and back. So I stay focused on love and serve as the example left by Jesus.

Just by loving my wife and putting her goals and ideas in play, guess who got a new set of golf clubs? Yep, you got it the man who loves and respects his wife. Our children honor and respect their parents not out of fear but love. The love we showed them by our selfless love of putting others needs in front of our own. Yes. New golf clubs. Now that is awesome.

Take your commitment seriously, that is what marriage is about. Living your life for the benefit of others (family) through love with no conditions. Your wife is transformed in love as she is loved unselfishly by her husband. The family is also transformed for generations to come if the husband, father, and man just simply love unconditionally.

The best advice is to get a understanding of Jesus and the way the world was designed for man and woman to become husband and wife, raising children in unselfish love in a world designed by our creator intended us to live. And don't be over the top. Be loving, understanding and open to others where ever they may be in their own life journey. Your life example speaks volumes in all areas of your life. This my friends is what I wish I would have been told. Or better yet I wish I would have listened better about the truth of life example.

The information on FLRs is all over the board. Yes you must read learn about all aspects and even experience different elements. Finally as you flounder around in all these life choices hopefully the choice to love unselfishly will be the ultimate choice.

Loving FLR Makes Our Journey Complete

I am a devoted husband 53 years old I live in Florida and I maintain lawns for a living. For fun and pleasure I like to serve my wife, be a good father, read, play golf, and garden. Been married 24 wonderful years to a woman I don't deserve but love and adore more and more every day.

We are empty nesters learning to love each other again. The FLR concept has guided me to better understand my role as a supportive, loving and obedient man. With the insights I have gained about living in her world, the way she views things has opened a sensational element in my life unexpected but so rewarding. It is as if I have exploded in love and devotion for her.

My whole life I was always instructed to respect and honor women as a gift from God. My commitment in serving her and the needs of the family have always been important. Daily chores, shopping, talking, being involved and loving the time we have together always been part of our life. Studying Loving FLRs gave me the understanding of her thoughts and concerns in a way where it relates to our path in the journey together. The establishment of our Loving FLR makes our journey complete, with a purpose and great rewards. She says I am the greatest husband and father in the whole world. And she loves me with all her being.

Just this week she was visiting her sister and her family for the graduation ceremonies as we all attend in this life. It was our anniversary weekend of 24 years. By learning to listen to her through the FLR concept I was able to relax and not try to steal the thunder of her family getaway and make it all about me as the old person would. The ability to see that I should put what she deems as important first; being there for her family.

The ceremonies took place and finished and they had a great time I heard. After the graduation party was over during the last few days of her stay with her family I sent her my gift of love, a dozen roses. It reignited and sparked the vision of how awesome she is to those around her and to her in way that she would like it to happen.

The FLR concept is all about being in a loving and committed relationship. As a husband who serves his wife and family's needs for years. It gives me great hope that knowing I have showed my love and devotion to my wife to others and to my family. The reward is support of her vision of a successful relationship. Rewards for me are up to her, whatever that might be I am sure I will love it.

SECTION 2

His Attention to Detail Makes Him a Great Partner

Hello! I am 28 years old and I am a travel nurse so I've been able to live and work in several different places in the country. I'm a woman with a lot interests! I love running, working out, doing outdoor things and trying new activities. I also like to sing and play guitar.

For the longest time I've never had a successful relationship. But when my now husband told me about the concept of Loving Female Led Relationships - I was blown away! The more I learned I thought about it I realized that this was what I was wanting and needing my whole life. What sold me on the idea giving it a real try was when I opened up to him and said I didn't think I was ready for an exclusive relationship but I really liked him. He said he'd be totally OK with me seeing other men if I wanted to. I knew I found a keeper.

We are both home most of the day. I only work 3 days a week and he can do his job from anywhere, which is why it works out so great with my travel nursing. We share house chores for the most part but he always cleans the kitchen and bathrooms, basically because he's good at it. We never really organized it in any way but he always does what I ask of him and I help when I can. He knows that I get anxious about clutter and disorganization, so he likes setting my mind at ease.

Any time after I come home from a 12 hour hospital shift he always makes sure I'm coming back to a peaceful home, which I appreciate a lot. Usually he makes me a drink and even rubs my feet on the couch as we talk about the day.

Sometimes when I go on a date I might bring the guy to our home and my husband will have a small snack and make us drinks and then leave us be. This shows me that he cares about me having a great time and it shows how secure of a man he is.

My husband has always loved, adored, respected and revered powerful and confident women. Heck, he was raised by one. Also his independence and attention to detail makes him a great partner. He knows so many of the little things like how I like my coffee and how I like our bed made just as much as he remembers the bigger things like my twin sister's death anniversary and realizing when I need space.

I feel like I am a much more confident and happy woman. It's helped me realize a lot of my dreams. The biggest benefit by far is truly having a relationship on your own terms. When someone - especially a partner - recognizes you as a powerful woman or Goddess(!) it can make you more powerful. The biggest challenge I'd say is a tie between both of us becoming comfortable to be fully "out" about our Loving FLR and find a way to correct his behavior when I need to.

I'm always proud of my FLR. But one time in particular some guys we knew at my brother in law's wedding were teasing my husband and calling him things like "Mr. Mom", which is weird because we don't have kids but whatever. Finally when we were leaving the reception a drunk groomsmen said my husband wasn't a really man and he could show me what a real man was like.

Without thinking I quipped back, "How many of you can make a powerful woman happy as long as he has?" They all fell silent! It felt kind of liberating. I can't stand bullies, especially drunk ones. I couldn't keep from smiling.

A time recently where I felt really proud of his domestic skills and him being Mr. Mom is when we had a house warming party with girls that I work with and some neighbors. My husband cooked, made drinks and even did dishes. I helped at many points of course, but he really took charge of the whole event. Many of the ladies were impressed and complemented us the entire evening. Some even said they wished their boyfriend or husband were more like him. You can't imagine how proud I was.

Ladies, before starting a Loving FLR make sure you've shed at least some of the shame our society puts on confident women, it can be hard to lead a relationship while still carrying that.

I wish I had known about Loving FLR's sooner! More women would pursue them if they only knew!

Our FLR is the Beginning of the Best Years of Our Marriage

My husband and I were high school sweethearts. We married late in our senior year and had our first child two years later. Flash forward almost 40 years... our two children are grown and on their own. Even though it is just him and I now, I kept finding myself feeling like a hamster on a wheel spinning around trying to keep up with the seemingly never ending housework, laundry, making all of our meals, doing all of the shopping and trying - mostly unsuccessfully as I'd be too tired at the end of the day - to snatch moments of free time for myself - all while working full-time as a banker.

Through the years, my husband has been dropping hints about an FLR lifestyle that I didn't pick up on then. Things like, "There is a way you can have everything you want and have all of the leisure time you want." We even dabbled a time or two with the fantasy of him being my "slave" - and failed miserably. I didn't want a slave. I wanted my loving, caring husband.

Looking back he had been doing little things all along that pointed to an FLR lifestyle like making my coffee and turning down the bed covers at night. While I certainly enjoyed those things, I just didn't realize he wanted me to lead him or that I wanted to be the leader. Of course as they say, hindsight is always 20/20.

Three weeks ago he started doing things for me around the house. One night it would be dishes, the next he swept the floors. He became so attentive to my comfort - the first night he rubbed my feet I about lost it - the feeling was both exhilarating and so very, very sensual. His attention awakened me in ways I never, ever would have imagined.

The following weekend I awoke to my coffee made and a letter that began, *"Dearest Kim...Welcome to a very special day of enjoying your hobbies, long talks with girlfriends and being spoiled by your husband! I have been excited all week anticipating the weekend. The past week has been some of the very best days of our marriage. I truly mean that. What I am trying to do is to steer you to a "Female Led Relationship" or "FLR". You've always wanted this position. I know that now from the reading I've done online in the past few days."* He added, *"I want you to seriously consider that I'm not talking about a temporary thing but rather a major lifestyle change in our lives. I am more sincere than you can imagine and you dearly deserve to be rewarded for the things you've done in the past like raising our family mostly alone and keeping our finances in order."*

He went on to give me suggestions - like making him lists of chores and teaching him how to do the laundry. He also reiterated that the past week had been amazing for him and for us. We hadn't had the slightest argument. His attention made me feel exhilarated, sensual, powerful...and deeply loved and cherished. We've been having many long talks and refining our relationship and its boundaries. And have totally embraced our loving FLR lifestyle. I truly believe, as does he, that we're beginning the very best years of our marriage.

The past few weeks I've been almost totally stress-free. And our home has never been cleaner or more organized. He's a super organizer!. He's learned to do my ironing and has both excelled at it and has totally enjoyed it. When I look in his eyes I see total contentment and his deep love for me. That just adds so much to my feeling that this is right for us.

I never knew this type of lifestyle existed let alone imagined us living it, but it is working! And we're both looking forward with great anticipation to the next 40 years and growing in our loving FLR. I hope our story will inspire others who are wanting to try this.

Should I Call Myself a Submissive?

I was wondering about the term 'submissive' in discussing the males in FLRs – I have always been uncomfortable with it – maybe I am in denial – but I am not sure it is the right term to define the men in this community?

- I am totally under my wife's authority and she makes all the major decisions in our family – usually after at-least conferring with me.

- I do not argue with her, talk back to her, or contradict/undermine her decisions.
- I now have altered my desires and personality to accept and conform to her likes and dislikes.
- I do what she tells me to do without debate or questioning it.
- I have learned to watch and love her interests, shows and books she reads (while still have some of my own).
- If she mentions she has to get something or do something I immediately try to see whether I can take care of it.
- When she tells me we have to reschedule an event or other intimate session because of her work, I try to show that it's ok and to not make her feel any guilt.
- I have become a total feminist following her lead, believe in it, support it, (not that I was ever against it).
- I understand she is the head of our household – even if sometimes she allows for me to play that part.
- I am ok when she sternly tells me that I have done something poorly or made a poor choice – which I then truly try to

        change, not do it again, – without
        needing kink discipline.
- I help my wife in many ways to support her career, support her family, help her figure things out when she needs it.

Even though I am all of the above, and she loves my new vigor and redefinition as her 'husband' – she really would not want to call me submissive. I think it's a term with the baggage of an S&M, fetish connection and meaning. What could a better word be?

The word is a Gentleman. A Gentleman is gentle with women and cares for them in a loving, respectful and insistent manner. I am not a submissive man, I am a Gentleman.

Men Have Unrealistic Expectations for a FLR

I am a regular guy leading a regular life. I have nothing against the traditional relationship and to be honest traditional relationships have been a major part of my life as I imagine they have been to many of those reading this.

About 15 years ago I was introduced to a FLR. I met her at a masquerade party by chance. We started dating and enjoying each other's company like most couples. She gradually started taking more and more control of the relationship. She took control in a subtle way. We would discuss doing something and she would make the decision as to how we go about it. She would ask me to do something for her in a respectful way. But I always knew she just wasn't asking. Because we got along so well I never had a problem with her 'take charge' approach. When two people care for each other it shouldn't matter who is in charge. I was totally comfortable with it. It felt totally natural. It was one of the most loving relationships I've had the pleasure of being involved in.

It is the misconceptions of a FLR that I think stigmatize those who seek it. Mention an FLR to most people and images of a woman clad in leather whipping a guy in diapers. FLR is not about that. A FLR happens when a man and a woman comes to the realization than they're happiest with her being the authority. It doesn't necessarily have to do with any particular kink.

Not every man is a leader and not every woman is a follower. I found being in a FLR allowed me to be the kind of guy I truly am. I love women. I love being a gentleman. I love being there for the woman I care for. I've always believed that it takes a very confident man to be involved with a dominant woman and not feel intimidated or threatened. It takes a very intelligent man to realize the benefits of having an intelligent, dominant woman in his life who loves him. It shouldn't matter if she's the boss. I don't mind saying that I think it's not only sexy for a woman to be the boss in a relationship but more natural as well. Ever since I was a teenager I've always been attracted to strong, intelligent, dominant women.

By now you've noticed I haven't used the term "submissive.' Most dominant women aren't any different than women who are not dominant. They want all the same things that any other woman wants. The only difference is they prefer to be the boss. A dominant woman wants to be able to decide what direction her relationship will go. She stills wants a guy to be intelligent and make a lot of the small decisions and to be able to discuss things with her like any other couple but the big decisions are usually hers.

Be smart and realistic of your expectations. Too many guys think that FLR has to do with constant kink; that it means that the woman has to be constantly giving orders. Not true. For one thing there's this thing called life that you have to attend to as well. Secondly, giving someone orders constantly would be like having a second job. These are unrealistic expectations.

A man should expect to put forth the effort in getting to know a dominant woman like he would any other woman. Get to know what she likes and doesn't like is part of the process of her taking control and him accepting that. Accepting what she likes and how she likes things done is the basis of participating in a FLR.

Life Was Good With Sandy Running Things

I first got involved in a Female Led Relationship by accident. My wife and I were living in Hawaii when she lost the ability to walk. It started slowly, first I did all the shopping. She would write out a list and I would shop. Before driving home, I would call and ask what I could bring home for lunch. Sometimes it would be take out, sometimes it would be something for me to cook when I got home, sometimes I would surprise her with shrimp for shrimp cocktail. She loved bacon and tomato, or grilled cheese sandwiches. She didn't like lettuce!

I would move her out to my garden on house cleaning day. She looked like a queen in her peacock chair, surrounded by flowers and I loved watching her. On laundry day, I would drive into Pahoa early, park right out front and get the best washers. While the clothes were in the wash, I would walk down to the corner cafe for a Bloody Mary. One morning, one of the regulars told me I was P---- whipped, that my wife should be doing laundry. I explained that I loved her, and I just put up with him. After putting the clothes in the dryers, I would have a beer and get a half order of eggs Benedict to bring back home to Sandy since she loved eggs Benedict.

I bathed Sandy every morning, and washed her hair. I enjoyed every moment of doing for her. In the afternoon, I would walk the dog, the walk took around an hour, but being in Hawaii, I would bring Sandy a beautiful bouquet of exotic flowers since they grew by the side of the road. My life was good with Sandy running things. I had never been more content. Sadly, Sandy passed from heart failure in 2012. Now I only go with dominant, take charge women! I highly recommend a FLR to any man who values a happy life!

I Am the Support Spouse

I didn't start off looking for a FLR but over the years I ended up in one. My wife just happened to have the traits that naturally led her to a FLR. I suppose I did too. I was more willing to submit to her will.

But specifically, the sacrifices I've had to learn are, she's in charge. Her wishes goes. Financially, she is the breadwinner and she took over the finances. It's hard to lead when your partner is making the money. I think that was the main realization that led me to understand that I was the support spouse. The housework is mine to do along with most of the cooking too. The child rearing has also fallen primarily on my shoulders.

Two other areas that come to mind are, how she demands certain behaviors from me. If she doesn't get them, there is a lot of verbal correction. She has used it in public on occasion. It doesn't bother her to show people that she is the boss. That also reinforces our roles to me.

Appearance wise, I realized that I had to take better care of how I look. She would often comment on how I looked like a bum, or my clothes made me look fat. I tended to wear baggy clothes for the sake of comfort. I didn't always shave in the morning. Now I shave every day.

I don't wear unflattering clothes anymore. I started wearing my clothes with more coordination in mind. I also took advantage of the new fashion trend for men, to wear leggings, sports tights, whatever you want to call them. I always wear a shirt long enough, so as not to be distracting. More often than not, I tend to be the one in tights, while my wife wears jeans. We've been out in public this way. It's a partial reminder to me of who is wearing the pants in the relationship. But I think it also signals to others that FLR are becoming the norm. That men can learn to be comfortable wearing the "tights" while women lead comfortably wearing the "pants."

I know what you're thinking. It's a kink. It's really not. It just so happens that leggings are comfortable. They're available to men. Most choose not to wear them. I do. But it helps symbolize to me that I'm not the stereotypical leader of my relationship. To some judgmental others, they might think, well we know who wears the pants in that marriage. Well even if they thought that, they would be right. I don't have to feel uncomfortable if my wife chooses to verbally correct me in public. I'm already showing that I wear the tights.

So there are some of the sacrifices I had to make. I prefer to think of them as adjustments from stereotypical gender roles. It's just my role in a FLR. My wife comes first, and I am the support spouse.

My Loving Support is its Own Reward

Towards the end of a week of self-obsessed surfing I recently had the good fortune to stumble across the site called Loving FLR and the sister site Conquer Him. Now in my early 60s and retired I have always kept my desire to be led by a woman to myself. Thanks to my furtive explorations down the years I was well aware of the existence of femdom, which was never an option, but had never before come across the concept of Loving FLRs.

Seven years ago my first marriage ended, with the final ten years free of intimacy. Six months later I was in a new relationship with a partner who loved to make love. She took the lead on an adventurous and exciting journey during which I was happy to follow. For the first three years we were in a long distance relationship but three years ago I retired and moved to be with my partner who was, and is, still working. As the one with time on his hands I cooked most of the meals, took care of the laundry and was happy to be supportive in whatever way I could be.

Not long after, the menopause kicked in. At first this was a difficult transition for my partner but she has coped with it exceptionally well. However, the change in our love life was a challenge. While researching the menopause I came across a wonderful book by Joan Price, about sex for the over 50s, written for couples but from a women's perspective, which then led on to her website. With great nervousness I told my partner about the book. I needn't have worried because she was delighted to hear something positive about this stage of her life. Following guidance from both book and website we have introduced the idea of "The Sunday Date" as a special time for ourselves. Meanwhile, thanks to the book, I was also able to tentatively suggest some variation to our play. Several months later I was invited to let her know what my needs might be.

It was this invitation that led to my week of self-obsession that began with being all about me and my desires. Thankfully, before the end of the week, I had arrived at the sites of Loving FLR and Conquer Him which provided me with the guidance I needed to reorient my focus. I was now able to concentrate on the needs of my partner and the ways that I could best support her further than I had done to date.

She has just begun a new job alongside the additional stress of supporting her ageing mother, all the while coping with the menopause. By the end of the week that had begun with my selfish ponderings, I now had the confidence from Loving FLR and Conquer Him to reveal my desire to serve a Powerful Woman and to suggest that I intended to do much more to be positive and supportive in order to remove as much stress from her life as possible. Furthermore, the goal was for her to become empowered, to ask and expect me to undertake much more in order to make her life less stressful.

Of course, this was all new to her and it is still early days. I must avoid rushing things, especially as the aim is to reduce stress, not add to it. But we have inaugurated another special day called "Her Friday Treat" where the center of attention is my partner, from her choosing the meal that I will prepare for her arrival home to her relaxing on the sofa while I clear the kitchen. The evening his hers to pursue for her own pleasure. I now accompany her on shopping trips for clothes with a positive disposition, happy to follow from shop to shop and to carry her bags. Now that things are in the open, I go about my day carrying out tasks happy in the knowledge that this loving support is its own reward. It feels like we are stronger than ever, embarking on a new loving journey, navigating this new phase of our lives as we enter the 3rd Age.

I Was Living in a Fool's Paradise Until I Met Tiffany

I was in a stereotypical relationship with my Wife because my upbringing was such that I was always given to believe that the man should be leading the relationship. I too was always under the false notion that a man is happy with this arrangement. This was my male ego speaking but I was wrong. I was never really happy in life and I felt I was missing something.

One day at a party which I attended alone I was introduced to a very pretty and charming girl named Tiffany who was half my age. During the course of our conversation I got around to bragging about the superiority of males. She just smiled and said I was wrong and that I needed to be trained and educated in matters relating to relationships. She was very well versed in matters related to Female Led Relationships and sex in general. She explained to me in minute details as to how and why Females are naturally superior to males in all respects right from a Woman giving birth and life to a man and how She nurses him and nurtures him and makes him strong. She rightly explained to me that right from birth a man has always been dependent on a Woman for everything. When small he depends on his Mother for everything and then when he grows up and marries he is completely dependent on his Wife for every single thing.

She explained to me that if left on their own, men would not be able to do anything. She told me that behind every successful man there is a Woman who guides him and who points out his mistakes and who corrects him in what he does. She then told me that however old a man may grow in age he will never grow beyond the age of 12. She told me that men are like children who need to be checked and reprimanded all the time. She proved to me that Woman can multi-task whereas men cannot. She told me that Women can endure greater physical pain whereas a man would never be able to bear pain such as pain at childbirth. She told me that Girls mature much earlier than boys and that was enough proof of Women being superior to men. She gave me lots of evidence of Women being superior than men and I couldn't counter Her charges in any way because when

I reflected on them I realized that every single word that She said was entirely true.

I was living in a fool's paradise until I met Tiffany. I felt like all this time my eyes were covered with a thick black band and She opened my eyes. She enlightened me and guided me properly. She destroyed my useless so called 'male ego' and male arrogance. I was ever grateful to Her for educating me.

From then on I had always wanted to be living in a Female Led Relationship. I introduced Tiffany to my Wife and She too was highly impressed and convinced by Her words of wisdom and so from then on my Wife took charge of our relationship although She was initially reluctant to do so when I had explained it to Her before meeting this Wonder Woman Tiffany.

It was all thanks to Tiffany that now I am very happy living in a FLR relationship. I believe that the world will definitely change for the better if all men in our society embrace Female Led Relationships. There will be no disgusting wars and pain and misery and poverty. There will always be Peace and Harmony and the world would definitely be a better place to live in. I feel that now that I've learned the facts of life from this beautiful Woman Tiffany, I could help in spreading this way of life to all, which in fact I am doing right now. I try to educate Women and men about the great benefits of adopting the FLR way of life. Thanks for giving me this opportunity.

I Introduced FLR with a Letter to My Wife

I mentioned to my wife the other day about Female Led Relationships. I pointed out to her that for the most part our relationship has been female led. Most of the major decisions in our lives together were her decisions.

For example, when we met at college, we started dating four months before I graduated. We met in Kansas. I was from New York, she was from Minnesota. I was a senior and she was a freshman. In March, two months before I graduated, she told me she was coming to New York with me after I graduated. I thought she was not thinking clearly and said so. She decided to give me the silent treatment for a while. I could not bear to have her silent towards me and after two weeks I agreed that she should come to New York with me.

We were engaged on her birthday, July 22, 2001, and married on August 10, 2002. Fast forward to 2008, that summer, my wife met her birth mom, they hit it off so well, that my wife decided that we should move to Minnesota so she could be closer to her birth mom. So, four months later, we moved to Minnesota. Moving on to recently, I mentioned it to my wife that we were pretty much in a Female Led Relationship. I even gave her some links that she could check it out. She agreed that she pretty much leads in the relationship. She also said that she didn't have a lot of confidence. She does want to learn more and push forward with being in control and taking charge of the relationship.

Leading up to our anniversary, I wrote her a letter expressing my devotion to her, and what I needed to do to better her life. For example, I need to do more chores around the house. I also said I needed to be more respectful towards her. I also said I needed to take better care of myself. With her leading, it should be her control on everything. She acknowledged a while ago that she could not handle the finances. Since FLR was brought up, I asked her for control of the finances. It turns out that she really liked the letter I wrote.

She went away for the weekend and she left me a note telling me what she expects me to do while she is gone. She really is happy that I came across FLR, and we have seen positive changes in both of us since I first mentioned FLR to her.

I Practice FLR with Married Women

Thank you very much for putting together the **Becoming an Anchor Course for Men.** Thank you so much for your guidance and good humor with it! I have gained a huge insight from this and I am confident that my interest in FLR for the last five years is now about to shift up a gear!

I have always loved and respected women and it feels as though it is my duty to serve them as the superior gender.

I am very fortunate because I have married women in my life who love their husbands and families who are happy to allow me to practice on them with dating but no sex. Their husbands approve of the arrangement which is wonderful.

It is a perfect situation and I cannot believe that these situations are becoming available to me. It feels as though these beautiful women know something about the shift in me just by looking at me.

The story starts with the fact that I am currently with the most gorgeous woman in the universe. Her name is Jackie and whilst she has found me very attractive, she told me at the very beginning of our relationship/friendship that I was too old for her and that our situation was unsustainable long term.

The truth is that I am 66 years of age and she is 46. She told me that she wants someone her age to live out her life with. She remembers the exact date she first noticed me four years ago and she says that she has been very fond of me since that date. She was trying to reverse her car with a trailer on behind and was having difficulty. I offered to help and she accepted. She was in an eight year relationship with a man who treated her badly in the end and that relationship finished about a year ago in very difficult circumstances.

The loving between us is extraordinary and while I have discussed FLR with her in a very small way she spoke to me about Equality. This was very early in the relationship. What happened is nothing short of amazing for me. She invited me to stay in her house on the evening before we were to go away motorcycling together. She offered me her bed and that she would sleep upstairs in one of the beds that her sons usually use. They were away with their father on this particular weekend.

I opened up to her and said that I really did not want to be on my own in the same house as her and in her bed, would she please allow me to cuddle her in her bed.

She told me that this is not meant to happen, but she conceded and joined me. Prior to this she had cooked me tea and we chatted and had a couple of glasses of wine. It was a very beautiful experience and we had the nicest weekend together away riding motorcycles in the Snowy mountains of Australia.

One thing that has become apparent during the last five months since that first night together is that we communicate and talk and listen to each other beautifully. I read to her and she loves it when I do that. I actually serve her as I would an FLR wife and when she comes to my house I cook for her, prepare the house, get flowers in for her and often write little cards for her. We have developed a routine where I write her an email every morning that she reads at the beginning of her day.

She works hard, has a demanding career and has two teenage sons who live with her. She gets every second weekend off and we are free to spend time with each other at either her place or mine. She does not always respond to my text messages or my emails but my approach to that has been to Honor her Choices and to try harder to become irresistible to her without being demanding.

No matter how neglected I feel when we are apart which is during the week except for fitness training at a gym, together on Monday and Wednesday nights, it is always perfect when we are together and when she calls me. I have experienced some anxiety that this beautiful relationship seems destined to end when she is ready and she seems to be preparing me for that eventuality. However, current body language when we are together doesn't seem to match the words, but still I want to Honor her Choices.

The friendship and communication in this relationship is the best I have ever experienced in my 66 years and I have been married twice and had numerous relationships with very beautiful women. Recently I attended a seminar and I have come to realize that my expectations of her were unreasonable, given that she has remained steadfast in her view that I am too old for her. In these seminars there are some very beautiful and friendly women, the married ones seem to be the most self-assured and attractive.

What I have found is that part of my new found confidence is to be very open about what I am feeling and last week I approached a woman named Sandra and told her that I really liked her and that I would like to befriend her. At that point I didn't know that she was married, or that she has four boys aged from 5 to 11 years old. She works with her husband in his practice and obviously loves him so my respect for her is about forming a friendship that is non sexual from the beginning. I asked if she was interested in dating me and she said straight out if I am ever in her city to please call her and we can go out for coffee or a meal.

Yesterday I hosted a visit by another beautiful woman called Robin, her husband Luke, and their two 16-year-old daughters. They are all beautiful people and I made pizza for them for lunch from my wood fired pizza oven. I make the dough and do the whole bit through to cooking and service.

I gave them a tour of my property and showed them my last twenty years of passionate work with photography. We are going to meet for dinner at Robin's suggestion. I asked if Sandra could join us and it's a yes. Robin's daughters seem enthusiastic about the dinner date as well. I feel very special at this point.

Back to the fact that Jackie's apparent indifference about a long term relationship seems to be less important now that Sandra and Robin seem to like me for my openness. Robin is going to teach me Mindfulness and Sandra will give me great opportunity to practice the skills that I want to use to become irresistible to Jackie! So what has come out of this whole recent experience is that I feel less anxious about my ability to attract and to serve and in fact I am proud of my life and my achievements.

Jackie has emphasized that I am the best lover she has ever had, like head and shoulders above. You can imagine how nice that is for a man who should be past his prime! I can tell you that recent business developments are giving me a huge boost to my self-esteem and it is incredibly humbling to see the results from these developments filtering through as enthusiasm for life. Meditation has been part of my life since 1999 and I do feel much less ego driven and so humbled by the opportunities that I have been given. In 2005 I was diagnosed with Bowel cancer and I have had more than ten extra years of life since operations and treatment for that disease.

The FLR theme feels strong in my life and it is not because I want to subjugate myself or be without responsibility. I want to assume more responsibility if anything and make her my Queen. When I can do that I become her King! It is more because I want the woman who chooses me to really shine and be involved in life alongside me. In the end it will probably be a lower level FLR that prevails but it is up to the woman really to make the final decision about that.

My Goal is to Help Her Be the Best She Can Be

Let me tell you a little about my wife as she's exceptional. Not only is she really smart (has two doctorate degrees in health care) but she is really driven to do her best. Her work ethic is at a very high level and she truly cares about her patients (when practicing) and her students (when teaching). Moreover, she's classy in every way and she's a great mother to our four kids. Most importantly, she has great faith, ethics and morals. She has changed my life for the better in so many ways. She was the reason that I became a Catholic and I'm so glad that I did. She keeps me on the straight and narrow – wives are good at that.

In college, she was a nationally ranked gymnast and I really think that competitive spirit has influenced much of how she operates – i.e. be your best, work hard, set high expectations. I'm not afraid to say that early in our marriage I was intimidated by her successes on all fronts. She had a much better resume than me (still does), was out earning me (although not any more) and was very vocal on her expectations of me and our marriage. I really don't think that she meant for this to happen but her strength and attitude certainly contributed to turning me into a supportive husband. I was always so desperate to please her and win her over that I became driven to serve her. I'll admit that I've had passive tendencies since I was a teenager and have always been in awe of the female gender but her forcefulness and ambition in the first several years of our marriage set off a mindset for me that has not changed since. My wife is superior, she knows it and I have to keep her happy. Hence as part of my desire to please her, because of necessity and because I have some nontraditional tendencies. I became what I understand every wife needs and many want-- a wife. Once it started there was no turning back and I would be lost in another role.

How did this evolve? My wife was working and going to school while our kids were young. She was trying to do it all (as they say), including the housework. She was and still is somewhat old fashioned. It was planted into her mind that it was the wives job to care for the home whether she worked or not. But she needed help and I was the answer.

I can't really remember how the transition went but I've been doing 100% of the cleaning, laundry and grocery shopping for the vast majority of our 29 years of marriage. For years she reluctantly agreed. She didn't buy into me assuming what was once (still?) viewed as a feminine role in our home and she was critical of how I did the work. Fast forward years later, she's accepted the role. It's now expected that I would do all of the housework. She's even bought me birthday presents that are geared towards being a homemaker. Her sister knows what I do. She doesn't like to broadcast to the world that I'm the domestic but she gives me chores as if it was as natural as could be.

Doing virtually nothing at home allows her to be the best that she can be professionally and boy is she good at what she does. This freedom allows her to pursue other interests. She loves to read, exercise, go on hikes, volunteer at church, etc. I, on the other hand, am very comfortable to be in a support role. I was made to be a homemaker even though it will never be more than a part-time role. But there's more. My wife doesn't have an office staff set up like I do. She needed a secretary and I was chosen. She saw that I was very task oriented and really organized. She's brilliant but a bit scattered. She knew that I wanted to please her. So she turned me (actually, I applied for the job) into what is essentially her personal assistant. Because of our roles in the marriage I was completely on board.

Not many days go by that my wife doesn't ask me to do something. Print this paper. Make this phone call. Run this errand. Remind me to do this. I need nylons – she doesn't even need to tell me what size or shade. Order me this dress. Return this to the store. Hang up my clothes. My legs are sore. I'm out of eyeliner. Renew my license. Make a reservation for my trip. It's constant and completely natural for her to give me to do's and she knows that I will do exactly as she says --and guess what? I want to.

I am a partner in my firm. I get more satisfaction out of serving my wife than I ever would at work. Work is work. Serving my wife is my passion. Just the other day she said that I need you to take a Friday off soon as she was planning a get together for a couple professional women at our home on a Saturday. Amazingly, she didn't have to explain at all. She knew that I knew this meant I'd be cleaning the house on Friday and running errands all day for food preparation, etc. The chemistry is there. Some men would disagree but I believe that when your wife has a real sense of power position in the marriage, it makes the husband so happily weak (in a good way) that he can't and won't say no. My wife has that power over me. She couldn't be nicer but yet she completely controls my emotions.

It's often said that wives/mothers have a lot of guilt. Well I did/do to. I started doing the housework when my wife was working on getting her masters/PHD and working as well. Once I started, I never stopped. She knows it has to be this way. She doesn't say it but there's no way she would change our roles, other than she would like to work less. She's starting to notice that we're not alone. She mainly just laughs and compares now to the past. She doubts that the men of a generation before me would actually be happy to be a "housewife." She knows I'm different but she knows that I make her life easier.

If I may gloat a little more about my wife. She's getting both a national academic and local athletic award this summer. I know that the only way she can do what she does outside the home is for me to relieve her of just about all responsibility inside the home. I just love catering to her needs. It may be hard for most to imagine but I get excited when she tells me to do something. Despite her successes I'm still the main breadwinner so I work really hard too. I average about 600 hours of overtime per year. But my work doesn't stop when I leave the office. Saturday is typically cleaning day. Sunday is grocery day. Weeknights include laundry and errands. I pack my wife (and my youngest daughter, who is still in high school) a lunch every work day. It's a full schedule but the housework doesn't stress me and I've gotten good at it. Occasionally my wife will tease me that I should get a second job doing it for other women. If I had a choice financially, I would quit working and serve her 24/7. God willing and if I'm healthy, that will be reserved for when I retire.

So I've shared a lot. It's hard for me to speak for how my wife would tell her story. She would probably say it's a mixed bag. She truly appreciates what I do for her. She needs me to do what I do for her. She still likely has some guilt that her husband does all the housework so she's reluctant to share it with the world. It took a long time but I think she's over the concern that I'm playing a female role. She's sees that society is changing and that I'm not the only one. She's amazing in so many ways and I like to believe that I've played a small role in her success. She always has been and always will be the "boss" and I'm very accepting of my role in our marriage. After 29 years, I think it's working. I often wonder, should I tell the world or is the world not ready for a man like me?

My Feelings for FLRs Are Like an Addiction

I don't talk about the FLR subject much outside of with my wife, of 29 years, except for an occasional comment to the ladies at work that I'm the domestic and/or that she's the boss. There's still a fear in me that if I truly open up on how I absolutely love being subservient to my wife that people will think I'm weird. Being how I'm wired, I do notice all of what's going on around me though. I'm convinced that women one by one and year by year are slowly taking over. What? Everything.

My wife is more traditional. We have four kids, we're both successful professionally and we have close ties to our Catholic faith. She resists some of the role changes that are taking place but she tolerates my ways. She hasn't done housework/laundry/grocery shopping of any type for at least 20 years and she'd happily admit that I'm like her personal assistant. She's pretty busy so the need is real and rarely does a day go by that I'm not asked to do something. That said, she's not 100% on board with the FLR concept but also no longer says that I married a man and not a woman, as she did in the early years of our role reversal. She is also coming around to how women are taking charge outside the home.

She's a professor and sees how women/girls are whipping the men/boys in education. Also, she has a healthcare background and actually believes that the environment is causing changes in men that stunt their desire to exert themselves. Her theory is that the mass use of birth control is causing estrogen to infiltrate our water system, it's being swallowed by men and causing some erosion in our masculinity. She's still old fashioned so she worries about a society full of wimpy men. That said, she sees how I support her career with taking away all tasks/organization in our home and I'm sure she would not want it another way. She's long past the guilt stage of me doing everything at home. I just wish she would more outwardly embrace her role as being in-charge.

For me, I couldn't even imagine being the boss and she knows it. I am the boss at work though. I often wonder how I got to be how I am and I think of instances in my life that may have triggered my brain to want to be bossed/led. The psychology of FLR truly fascinates me. I try hard to focus on the non-sexual aspects of being a sincere subservient husband but it's really hard not to want that side too. I'm not talking about anything hardcore, just things like her communicating to me and the world that she wears the pants. My wife says my feelings are like an addiction and maybe she's right but it enters my mind every day. I saw your post on the commercial with the guy doing laundry and being told to go to the store. I'm regularly in that position. My wife expects me to do all the housework but she doesn't hesitate to tell me when she's not satisfied. She's Italian and I get yelled at here and there. With her, it's like a subtle form of dominance. There's absolutely no question on who's the boss in our house but she alone decides when she wants to exert it.

So I'm already a fan of your approach/website and I look forward to learning from you and your readers. I've spent much of my adult life trying to show my wife the benefits of FLR. It frustrates me that were not on the same page but I love my wife for who she is and I'm grateful for when she does offer a tease or action. She does truly know that she has the power to really put me in her complete control but she largely holds back.

As for me, I'm not embarrassed to do housework, to say that I'm her servant (In a nice way), to admit that she rules the roost. It's all very natural to me. I suspect that the direction of women's leadership outside the home will cause future generations of men to have to accept a similar role, whether they like it or not. I always felt like I'm ahead of my time but very happy too!

I Was Hoping His Interest in FLR Was Only a Phase

I was introduced to the concept of Female Led Relationships by my husband. I came to realize he has had a desire for FLR for quite some time but was not able to come right out and discuss it with me. He read lots of books and websites and would show me some of them that grabbed his attention. I read some of them but must be honest and say that the ideas presented to me did not appeal to me at all in the beginning. I realize now that I was filled with a lot of fear and had a very closed mind about the idea of women being the dominant partner. I knew of a few women on Fetlife who were into it, but they were complete strangers and I couldn't imagine having much in common with them at all.

I was hoping this interest of his which seemed to have turned into an obsession was only a phase and would go away at some point, even though that did not seem very likely to be the case. I had two problems: I did not understand what FLR was and was not, and I didn't think it was anything "normal" people did. So I just kept pushing it away and wanting to know less and less about it.

What I was learning about FLR is that it was a lifestyle that involved turning myself into a FemDom and wearing latex clothing and stiletto heeled boots or the like. That was very scary because it just is not me. It probably is not most women. But I did have some experience with what a FemDom was like, because we dabbled on the edge of the BDSM community for a time and knew some FemDoms and heard them give seminar sessions at some BDSM events.

I have no desire to have anyone be my slave, and it really creeps me out to think about it. We have since stopped attending those events, but we do have a few friends who are really into it.

Eventually we found some websites that espoused less radical ideas that made more sense to me. We came across the Disciplinary Wives Club with Aunt Kay and watched one of the videos and decided it had some ideas that appealed to us. We saw a video which was an interview with an older couple who seemed much like us. So I began to feel very differently about relationships led by the wife.

At this time I do feel that I have what it takes to be the dominant partner. We both agree that I have am the better decision maker. I have started to take pride in my ability to lead. And as I look back at times when I tried to force him to make the decisions about things in the past, it did not work out that well, as he never felt comfortable deciding things. I have a good sense of what is good for the both of us, and I am coming to realize that there as many styles of relationships as there are people, so it is foolish to try to fit into a mold that is too traditional for our needs.

Also, another factor to be considered is that he has a strong feminine side that fits better in the role of following instead of leading. So it seems this would be a win-win situation for us. However, I have a lot to learn and much to do to build my confidence in leading. I am happy to be the chief decision maker, but at this point I do not feel comfortable being up on a pedestal. And I need more work erasing the idea that FLR is equated with FemDom, which really seems more about sexual fantasies than a 24/7 lifestyle.

We Are the Average Couple in a Female Led Relationship

'm Sam and my husband is Adrian and we have been married for nearly five years. We are one of the couples who participated in the FLR Couples survey and when we saw the results we had no idea how common certain details of our relationship were. After reading LovingFLR.Com for about a year now, we figure that it is about time we shared our story.

We had never even heard of Female Led Relationships until my husband expressed an interest in BDSM just to have a little more fun. We liked the idea of femdom and it was a lot of fun to play around with but it wasn't until Adrian stumbled upon LovingFLR.Com that we sat down and talked about it seriously.

He approached me to ask me if I wanted to explore more. It seemed fascinating that this could be an actual lifestyle instead of just play time during our love making. We read every single article on LovingFLR.Com and learned a lot. We realized that we can have whatever type of relationship we want as long as he honors my choices and is happy to do it.

He agreed that this is what he wanted. I will be honest after the shock of having things go my way, every time, I have adjusted very well. FLR has made me really have to sit and decide what I want from my relationship and my life in general because I can't express my needs to him unless I know what I want for myself.

My FLR boosted my confidence quite a bit as well. I trust myself to make the best decisions and I have completely stopped second guessing myself. My husband notices it as well and it makes him happy to see that I am direct and deliberate. We don't do any of the BDSM stuff anymore. We live out a regular life except when I want something done a certain way, I always get it.

Sexually he is not passive and his aggressiveness in bed is one of the reasons I married him so there is no sexual domination on my part in our relationship. We make love whenever we feel like it, he will initiate or I will. The only rule we set in place was that I would always peak before he could.

I am spoiled by him now more than ever before. I feel like he is my magic wand. He can do anything or take care of anything that I could ask for. Sometimes I challenge him with odd requests just to laugh as he scrambles to get things done. That's the kind of fun we have with it. Otherwise, we don't do anything ritualistic. We have fun together. We never argue. We don't have to. He asks me what I think or what I want and I tell him and that is it.

He is older than I am by 15 years but that doesn't bother us. He earns more income than I do. My income is mine to do whatever I please. I have more free time than he does so I tackle the housework because I enjoy keeping things in order myself. As such, I am in charge of the finances and we both get a small monthly allowance, everything else is put away.

He is such a type A personality; he just has to do a good and thorough job. It makes him so happy to do things for me and see me smile afterwards.

Focusing On Myself Helped Me Become a Goddess

I have known Alex since I was a child. We both grew up overseas and our parents worked together. We hung out as kids and his older brother is a good friend of mine. Alex is younger than me by 4.5 years. As we got older our paths separated and we both went away for University, careers, marriages. Even if our paths hadn't crossed for a long time, we always knew of the whereabouts of each other thanks to the great friendship our parents shared.

Anyway, seven years ago thanks to Facebook our paths met up. Of course now I can say it was meant to be. No one comes into our lives without a reason. Being attracted to each other and our special life long bond after we reconnected on Facebook we decided to meet up. It was the best day ever! After that day we shared a very intense year-long love affair. We tried to stay together but I was unhappy and so was he. He tried controlling me, my life, movements and I walked away unhappy, sad and with lots of pain.

We kept in touch and saw each other every now and then but it always ended in a negative way. At that point I took my life in my hands and started searching for what I needed to move on, break away from the standard living and expectations of others. I started putting my needs and desires first. I joined the Velvet Tent which was led by Kristin Morelli and her Red Tent Revival that stirred inside of me the power and desire to change, to reach out for more. So I checked the internet, started meditation and working on me and what I wanted for myself.

I have always been an assertive, smart woman. As Alex says, whatever I start, I finish well. This is true!

Anyway the distance and my focusing on myself changed me and allowed me to become the powerful Goddess I am. Alex liked the change. He has always been my LOVE and I know we belong together so I started seducing him slowly and with determination. He then admitted that he always wanted a powerful women who he could serve, he just wasn't sure I was willing. This of course is because we started slowly opening up our hearts to each other and telling each or what we really wanted.

Now as time passes and we are slowly moving back into becoming a couple. It is magic, sexy and so nice to be served. He allows me to freely express myself and grow and I give him the guidance he needs to led a better life.

Your website helped me to start to understand what I wanted and what I was truly looking for.   I came across this website by chance. Although sometimes I really don't think it was by chance. It has guided me into a world I knew little about and it has given me useful and correct information and enlightened me. I read every story and followed much advice you gave. I truly believe that living with Alex in a FLR is what is best for us even if each expresses our kinks. We see our kinks as sexy games that spice up our relationship and we both understand that even without them we would be a happy couple. I am happy, satisfied and so very pleased with my life and the direction I am going in.

I Support Her Career as Equally As My Own

We meet while at Grad School in Cambridge Massachusetts - from the beginning she was amazing - I saw her across an auditorium at our orientation the first day of classes. It was for me love at first sight!

For the first couple of terms She would be nice to me but her friends told her to stay away from me - I was 6 years older and had extensive work experience and maybe perceived with a bit of arrogance in my demeanor. I had been dealing with a number of deaths in my family and was at a very dark place in my life - that... I guess was a timely expensive therapy in architecture that I was able to escape into. We almost did not end up together be it for our last studio course we ended up in while both of us not placing it as our first choice. We became friends, then started dating, then became lovers, then she decided we would move-in together ... that's how it started I would say!

She was raised in the South in a very patriarchal Korean family. Being the oldest 'daughter', not going to medical school, attending a premier feminist women's college, and then deciding to become of all things an architect led to a bit of a falling out with her father to say it nicely. Her mother was always very proud of her and supported us when she could.

I was raised in the Midwest in the city of motors in a traditional Italian/Hungarian 'white bread' type of family ...fairly patriarchal as well. I was the baby with three older sisters. I learned many things from my father's traditional home but also how he deeply loved my mother. I also learned many things from my mother as well including laundry and folding, sewing, and cooking and We (my wife and I) were in many ways polar opposites. We were born in the same month but with her as a Leo and me as a Virgo we should not have clicked or lasted.

We moved back to my home city based on my contacts and connections and started a business together. It was not easy living in bombed out lofts and in a city that was about as low as it could get economically and spatially being derelict and rundown. It was tougher on her though - she would seemingly confront my past on numerous occasions. This was very hard professionally for a woman trying to make her way in a new city and in a field that was and still is male dominated.

Things came to a head one afternoon and our relationship changed subtly yet profoundly when she had enough and threatened to leave (having moved without us being married or engaged). She had a determined look on her face as she sat us down and began to ask what the hell we were doing. In not so many words she asked if I was ever going to propose to her and make us legit. I had been a typical male and quite oblivious to these matters and rather self-absorbed and in a matter of minutes, maybe an hour, the power dynamic with her and I subtly yet completely shifted to her having the real power in our relationship. I was in shock with some tears falling from my eyes, she stayed focused and dry eyed and I realized this had been bothering her for quite some time. I outweighed her by more than 100 pounds but knew that she had assumed control - to some level anyway. In many ways I look back at that afternoon and realized that was when the foundation was laid for our Female Led Relationship. I might say she maybe had been laying out the 'plans' so to speak when she decided we would first move in together during grad school.

We married soon after and things seemed to at some outward level return back to normalcy. She kept her last name, as did I. She began to find her way via teaching and excelled in this arena. And over the next decade we moved from renovated loft to renovated loft as her career grew in teaching architecture at the university level with my focus still in trying to carve out a fledgling architecture practice. She effectively was the main breadwinner with a stable prospectus and opportunities in her path. This sometimes was tough for me but also I saw her energized in the academic environment like never before.

We eventually had a child when she decided the time was right and became very close in a different way. Helping to care for the baby was amazing and I started to really help more around our home. I felt some level of guilt - not being all that I could have been as a husband at all levels in the past - and I wanted to begin to make amends. I became better at sharing the domestic duties and taking care of the baby. I fell in love with my wife all over again and started to change for the better as a husband. Amazing what a child adding to a couple can do!

We left the Midwest to head back to the east coast capitol district area based on both of our job possibilities and to start anew. Before we left I had one of her former college best friends come join us for a surprise ceremony to renew our vows... with her as a witness. It wasn't a formal FLR contract but I mentioned my intention to be a better husband, assuming more domestic duties, supporting her career and clearly mentioning loving, listing and deferring to her judgment. It at least for me was the framing of our new loving FLR - for her - she liked when her friend read the part in the vows at the end "that again we were married once again and that she can kiss the groom."

We continued on this path of building our surreptitious and somewhat stealthily FLR. I took a self-imposed vow of chastity (honor system) replacing my need for release with the joy, passion and new intensity of hers! It was amazing the first time I truly made her climax - we both became quickly hooked with this new connection and I do not believe we are ever returning to the old ways of making love!

We never really called it FLR or strove to take it towards 'femdom' or other more kink laden type of relationship. In my mind we were building a FLR - for my wife though she would not call it FLR but enjoyed the new me and at times bragged to her friends about my becoming a husband that does the laundry, helps to cook, does the dishes, majority of the cleaning and supports her career as equally to my own. Subtly and openly I had begun to become a feminist and really made strides to be better at listening to her at deferring to her judgment. This all was great - building our dream relationship while becoming ideal role models for our son to grow up in a home that was at least balanced - not really matriarchy yet but also for sure not patriarchy either. He would begin to see domestic/house work and chores not as "women's work" or for a "house wife" to stay at home and do but more as gender neutral and even if I must say as "man's work" based on my example. He would see both of his parents with professional careers but understand that it was really 'mommy' that was the boss.

This all was turned on its head when the recession of 2010/11 hit. My wife's job remained stable yet mine lead me to spend two years in living and working in Saudi Arabia apart from my wife and son. The things that life throws into your path can be really unfortunate yet there are almost always people far worse off than the troubles that we may have to face. Leaving a budding FLR and being immersed in the land of the polar opposite was a complicated and emotional 'dialectic' story for another time. Needless to say we survived my time 'In Kingdom' and picked up back where we had left off. That is to say until recently... another shift recently began.

Just last year my wife began to be courted by a major university to compete for a leadership position in their organization. It would be a major career move for her with the stability of tenure and pay now equaling my own. Her position would likely have potential to surpass mine making her on target to soon again the main breadwinner in our family. I viewed this opportunity for her as something that she deserved and earned. We decided together to begin this pursuit after she asked for my counsel and thoughts as we plotted this potential path. I knew it was going to happen and was delighted to support her however I could to give her the best chance for success. I would be able to move within my company so it was easy for me. In the end she was successful and we quickly uprooted and planted new roots with a fresh start based truly on her opportunities.

The first months were a complete shift in our lives with her going to dinners, social meetings, traveling and events - with me supporting her at all levels and flipping many roles we had assumed in our prior city. I was now dropping our child off and picking him up from school, I began making the majority of dinners with my wife taking over Sunday dinner, a task that used to be mine. I really enjoy when she ask/tells me I need to plan a dinner for her and her new colleagues (which has happened a couple of times so far). I also make sure lunches are made in the morning and make sure her dry-cleaning is ready whenever she needs it. Ten years back - I silently ask myself if I would have been able to deal with the switch in our roles... Maybe, maybe not, but look back and wonder if it was providence or was I just lucky to have my wife really Conquer Me long ago - and have had the practice and slow unfolding to become a feminist and male that enjoys both his professional work as well the domestic duties that have become my charge.

It's a new beginning and path that we are on relating to really wears the 'proverbial' pants better in our loving

Female Led Relationship - I think my mother would be mostly proud of how her son turned out.

I Am Happy Being a Servant to My Wife

My wife Jane and I dated in college, broke up, and got back together nearly 20 years later. She was rather shy, though sexually adventurous, and was intrigued by my desire to be of service to women. By the time we met up again, she had become a very successful executive.

Nearly a decade into our marriage, we hadn't explored the concept of a female led relationship, though I did share my fantasies with Jane. About five years ago, my brother Jerry married a beautiful younger woman, Nina, who brought FLR into our lives. We soon noticed that Jerry and Nina never fought and he immediately did anything Nina asked him to.

Jane and Nina soon became friends. They discussed FLR over wine at girls' night out. Nina was raised in the precursor to a modern FLR home. Her father was obedient to her mother. He was even deferential to Nina and her two sisters, generally following their instructions cheerfully. Nina absorbed the idea that men were to be respected, but women were to be obeyed.

Nina's father worked long hours as a doctor, but his office, at his wife's insistence, was only a few blocks from home. He was always available to take care of any task Nina's mother assigned him, or to take the girls shopping or to the movies. He was also responsible for all housework, including traditional cleaning, laundry, cooking, and grocery shopping.

Nina had grown up a bit spoiled but very independent and confident. Though nearly 20 years younger than Jerry, both knew from their first date that Nina would be the commander of their marital ship. Jerry delighted in giving Nina everything she wanted. He also took over many household duties to free his beautiful bride from boredom or drudgery.

Jerry works 60 hours a week, and makes a very good living. Nina doesn't work and spends her days working out, shopping, and having lunch with friends. She has expensive tastes, but always looks spectacular. Jerry is aware of the attention she gets from other men and isn't jealous. Indeed he considers the flirtation between Nina and her admirers a compliment to her beauty.

Jerry's world revolves around serving her. Many times he's gotten home late from a business trip and stayed up well past midnight grocery shopping, doing laundry or cleaning the house. Jerry also arranges several vacation and shopping trips each year for Nina.

Traveling to locations such as New York and London, Nina sometimes invites him along, and sometimes chooses to travel with girlfriends. So far, Nina has never invited a guy to travel with her, but it seems Jerry wouldn't mind at all. I think that, like me, he finds cuckoldry very exciting.

My wife came away from these discussions quite impressed. She isn't intrinsically "bossy" or dominant, but the lack of conflict was appealing. She liked the orderliness of Jerry and Nina's life. And, to be honest, she was a little jealous of the pampering Nina gets, along with her very generous budget. This gave me an opportunity to discuss **LovingFLR.Com**. Jane was relieved to learn she could be pampered and appreciated without pain, fetish play or other BDSM elements that she is uncomfortable with.

We began slowly, writing up a set of tasks that I would take over, and a few little acts of pampering that I promised to perform each day: breakfast in bed, foot massage at night, and at least an hour each evening set aside to be on call for anything she wanted. For me, it was a dream come true. And I could live my life openly, sharing with my grown sons, Jane's daughter, and Jerry and Nina.

Very quickly, we felt the conflict in our relationship diminishing. I was happy and fulfilled in the servant role I had always dreamed about. Jane felt cared for, attractive and energetic. She enjoyed having my undivided attention and obedience. Though I would love to have domestic discipline in our relationship, Jane hasn't yet felt it necessary. Our sex life improved. And we have begun to shift more duties to me and privileges to her.

We've become even closer with Jerry and Nina have become even closer to us. We've informally come to the point where both wives know they can expect obedience from both husbands. Just last week, I took Nina shoe shopping while Jane was at the spa and Jerry out of town on business. I handled his chores for him and felt pleasantly thrilled that I had been useful to Nina. The "goddess" concept began to sink in. I redoubled my efforts to devote myself to serving Jane and Nina. I often feel that I want to get on my knees and thank them both for the honor.

SECTION 3

It's Not about Being a Doormat or a Stepford Husband

The one thing I have learned is that every relationship is different - different Goddesses have different levels, wants and needs; god bless them all, they know better than we do, but it means that any advice given from a male point of view is subjective, so please take this as you will, and I genuinely hope that it helps you in some way.

My wife does not allow me to have male or female friends the same age. The main reason is was how I behaved when I returned - not rude or arrogant, but I carried myself with a certain "swagger".

She said it undone her hard work - I didn't know or realize the importance of that, but I do now. Switching off is wrong i.e. you can be the perfect, subservient husband/partner when she is there and around you, but when you are at work or away from her, your thoughts drift to other things and potentially masculine pursuits. This is understandable at first - all of us are only human after all, and the mind needs to be trained as well as the body. But, your first thought, in every, single life situation, should be - "Are my first thoughts and priorities with my Goddess?"

The people around you cannot only undo all your Goddesses hard work, but they can also bring you down and make you question who you are and what you are doing - men are born with a certain ego and a certain amount of pride. Let's be real, if you told another group of men that you were in a female-led relationship, you are very likely to receive some barracking - you might even receive a certain amount of joshing from a proportion of women. It is so important to forget every aspect of what other people think - one person, and one person only matters in your life. If you receive strange looks or people pass judgement on you, then smile, and explain that it is only your Goddesses opinion that counts.

This also counts when doing things, or putting yourself in certain situations which may be considered traditionally "feminine." I used to go to the pub every lunch hour, have a few drinks and wolf down some fast food on my way back to the office. Now, I have a lovely healthy salad with a jacket potato and go clothes shopping for my wife. This was very daunting at first, again, men are almost always raised a certain way, we are taught to abhor silks, satins, flowers, frills, lace, perfume and the like. Again, none of this matters or counts anymore; your life only counts from the first point that you became involved with your Goddess. It is easier said than done, granted, but in time, it should become almost second nature. By the time of writing, I don't think about it anymore - I have come to greatly appreciate ladies clothes and fashion.

If I go into a shop, I am more than happy to talk to the staff about colors, sizes, styles and accessories. I don't have to continually buy items (my wife controls my finances anyway) so I have to use my ingenuity or do what I normally do, take pictures of a pretty top that I had seen for instance and then send it to her.

Another instance was when we were playing Trivial Pursuit around a friend's house. If there is one bone of contention between us, it's the fact that I am very highly educated and hold a number of degrees, as well as being educated at Oxford University. My wife left school at 16 with no qualifications, primarily due to caring for one of her parents who had a long term serious illness. She is very naturally intelligent but doesn't quite have the confidence to push herself on. This can make things difficult at times.

While she is proud of me, she likes the fact that I have these things behind me, she finds it difficult being "superior" when I am the one with all the paperwork. I am naturally competitive. I always want to win. I always want to do well. One night, I did exceptionally well and won by quite some distance. I didn't think anything of it until my wife drove us home. I asked her if everything was ok and she told me in no certain terms that everything was not ok. I asked why and she said, "You work it out".

So I did. I realized that it is not about the winning, it's about maintaining your position and your respect. It isn't about letting her win either, its ensuring that she doesn't feel awkward or anything less than the Goddess she is.

If we play now, I say things like, "Well, my wife is so intelligent that I am sure she would know this one." If she doesn't know, I will say something along the lines of, "We all have gaps in our knowledge, and my wife certainly fills those gaps with her beauty." This is not for everyone, granted, but it makes her happy, and suddenly the game is secondary to her and far less important to me.

It's the same in public. You shouldn't "switch off" if you are doing something together. Share your devotion. If my wife buys a new item of clothing, I say something like, "My wife will look so beautiful in this," to the shop assistant. If I am accompanying her to the beauty salon, I would say something along the lines of, "My wife doesn't need beauty treatments, she is naturally beautiful and perfect in every way, but we all need pampering." Friends and family take a little more time, but again, you should maintain your stance, maintain your devotion. I was asked by a friend whether I still watched football for instance and I said, "I would prefer to sit and watch my beautiful wife all night."

In conclusion, it's not about being a doormat or a Stepford husband. My wife wants me to have character, she wants me to have personality, she wants me to be intelligent, but she also wants me to think of her first before anything, absolutely anything. Don't be hard on yourself if it takes time or if others bring you down. Smile and walk away knowing in your heart that somewhere, somehow, your Goddess will be smiling.

I Happily Took My Wife's Last Name

I'm sure that there are varying degrees of FLRs and what one Woman prefers is going to be different from the next. But one thing is constant: Her needs and desires come first, always, without question ever, at least in my relationship.

When I met my wife She was already a fully realized, in control Goddess who had no real need for a man in Her world. But I was so drawn to Her power and mindset from the first time we met, I couldn't let it go. Literally, I got on my knees, in public, and begged Her to go out on just one date with me. And guess what? She made me stay on my knees while She considered it, and even after She gave me Her answer (which was "yes, one date"), She wouldn't let me rise up until She out of my view. She later told me that it was my first humility lesson, and that if I'd have failed, that was it.

Anyway, long story short, after many dates and pleadings and a very real, rigorous 2 years of dating and then 2 years living together, She informed me we would marry and that I would take Her name. No hyphens - I have Her name. That was 5 years ago.

This may sound weak to You, but my world would fall apart without Her. I would not know what to do if She wasn't my everything. It sounds like She has much more control over my life than with other men in FLR's, but that's our way and it works for us both. There is plenty of love, and I live in accordance with Her rules and ways and there's never any strife because as You say in Your videos - She never makes a wrong decision or a bad one, She simply decides and leads, and I support and follow.

Our FLR Contract Worked Wonders For Our Relationship

My guidance could and does impact my partner. Throughout our relationship, he has made so many positive improvements to his life through my direction. Prior to our relationship and me coming and taking the FLR role without knowing that was what I was doing, he didn't have a lot of direction. Coming into his life, I made a lot of changes.

To make a long story somewhat short we got custody of his son. This was something he was not going to push for. I think based on my direction and the guidance I had with seeing the condition his son was in, that he opened up his eyes to what was going on and worked to get custody. This was at the beginning of our relationship and we still have custody. He now lives with us at 18. The biggest challenge we still face with that situation is the stepson's mother.

Subhub has also been more consistent in his jobs. He doesn't leave a job until he has another one. He has since become certified in his field and has been a much more positive influence in general on our lives. He is making an impact on what he does and is appreciated in his field. I am expecting that he will continue with furthering his experience in his field or adding additional certifications that will allow him to either move up or move on.

Currently, I am working with him to get him to control some of his baser instincts which do relate to sex and also related to anger and emotional variations. I have seen positive changes in his behavior. He has been significantly more respectful since we started our contract for our FLR. His spurts of anger have decreased. He is much more engaged in our discussions and in what we are doing with the kids.

I have found that since being in the contract, getting him to be more cognizant of the roles we interact in and he has really taken to the roles so much better than I expected. He follows through, he listens, and with everything written out, it is very clear. The biggest motivator for him is sexual so by using the punishment reward system in relation to sex, I have been able to see more progress from him in much less time than I was expecting it would take us to get there.

We Almost Went Our Separate Ways

It is a desperately hard thing for two people that deeply love each other, to accept that they have a problem which is likely to end with both parties going their separate ways.

I had been with my beautiful wife for three years after dating for around eighteen months. We were happy, very happy, but we used to argue a great deal - we are both very stubborn, we both have differing views on world issues, and neither of us deal with stress very well in all honesty. We coped reasonably well but life can throw you a lot of curve-balls at times. Our debt was spiraling, we worked different hours, one of our elderly relatives needed quite a lot of care for a time, all of which led us to arguing constantly, day and night, about everything.

Afterwards, we would often be in floods of tears, wondering why we were tearing each other apart when we loved each other so much. We had no answers, work/life constraints made it almost impossible for us to consider any possible answers, so things came to a point where we were making plans to go our separate ways. This was when we came across a documentary about surrendered wives, and then on the other foot, female-led relationships.

The comparisons to their marriages and ours were stark, almost unnervingly similar. Two strong-willed, strong minded, individual mindsets that frequently butted heads - it showed that it creates an atmosphere which is not only de-constructive, but where nothing is ever agreed or finalized, leading to all sorts of problems.

It showed that you are highly unlikely to maintain a relationship where two people have the same, stubborn mantra and that something has to change. Neither of us really thought we would get anything out of this programme, but it showed us where we were and that there was an alternative - the question was, who would step down?

Both of us agreed to write our terms for "leading", and show them to each other, and agreed to debate the matter in a civilized way without arguing. Being stubborn, I fully expected to win but it came very clear that my wife was in fact better than me at certain, crucial things such as managing money, as well as the fact that she spent a lot of her free time constructively and I couldn't really argue that spending time drinking down the pub and playing on my Playstation was a good use of my time.

So I agreed. It was a steep learning curve, steep as I have ever faced but things began to happen that I didn't expect. I didn't realize how much things were getting on top of me and what I was doing to seek an outlet for the stresses and strains of everyday life. After a time, all of those feelings fade into having one goal, one thought process - the only thing that should concern you is being obedient without question. I struggled at times, as anyone would, but it's a question of focus and accepting someone as your superior, in every way.

Several years on, we are enormously happy. She controls all our finances, I also dress her, bathe her, handle all the housework and continue to learn and be inspired by this amazing, beautiful woman. It's hard at times, but so is life. All I know is that our present situation is a thousand times better than it used to be, and we are physically fitter, healthier, wealthier and happier than we have ever been. A Loving FLR is not just a lifestyle choice, it can also be the solution to a great many issues. I am so pleased to be in service to my amazing lady, and I hope I can only improve and learn to do more.

Our FLR Is Our Treasured Secret

My Lady and I were introduced to each other by a mutual friend who knew us quite well and thought our natural Domina/submissive personas would be an interesting mix. We knew about each other, via our friend, for quite a while before we actually met. The chemistry was certainly right although she kept me at a distance for a few months until she was certain that my desire to serve her was genuine.

Her intelligence inspires and motivates me to this day. I've always felt comfortable around strong creative, confident women, preferably left-leaning, and my Goddess is all of that and more. Our relationship has endured because we enjoy discussing the nature of it often, finding ways to make it better. We've never let it stagnate, not for a day. I'm grateful that she has allowed me to be completely honest with her. It's safe for me to tell her what I need to. This comes with trust ...and probably time... and an abundance of feminine wisdom, which she has decided to share with me.

I did have a previous long-term FLR, although we didn't refer to it as that - and it was mostly during the pre-computer age, or early stages of it - and it was also her high intelligence that initially attracted me. I should also mention that we are still very good friends and I remain obedient to her, which she enjoys, although she uses her power wisely. I also want to say that I am writing this with my Goddess's permission and encouragement.

Although I'm certainly attracted to the physical beauty of a Goddess I am serving, it is without question her high intelligence that inspires me to serve her well over a long period. The erotic power of a dominant woman's creative intellect should not be underestimated. It's really the flipside of the spiritual power of the Feminine Divine, which I wake to every morning and am permitted to worship.

I might have mentioned this before, can't remember ... my earliest recollection of my true submissiveness to a supremely dominant woman - I would have been about 10 - was seeing Elizabeth Taylor in 'Cleopatra' ... I wanted to be one of the slaves serving her as if their lives depended on it, which, of course, they were.

My Lady prefers not to be titled Mistress largely because we don't live a Femdom lifestyle, at least not in the classic sense, and she feels that the title is more befitting of a Professional Dominatrix, which she isn't. She doesn't wear leather and she doesn't carry a whip. Such is her skill as a dominant leader she has no need for symbolism, affectations or costuming that she finds cumbersome, uncomfortable and completely unnecessary for eliciting my unconditional obedience, service and attentiveness. Mostly we simply call each other by our first names.

I am permitted to call her Goddess, which she loves, as it befits her position in our relationship and enhances her expectations that she will be served and worshipped by me. I use the title 'Lady', with her consent, as a special way of referring to her when writing about particular episodes of our FLR. I've told her that it keeps me reminded of her elegance and her wonderful feminine power and that I find it useful when writing about her. She has encouraged me to keep it. Her lover calls her mainly by her first name, although he does also use more traditional terms of endearment: Darling, Sweetheart, etc.

In public, with friends or strangers, we refer to each other by name. To loudly identify her as Mistress would kind of defeat the purpose of our FLR, which is to exist unobtrusively, out of the spotlight as it were. I think if we were out somewhere and we overheard, "Oh, look, they're in a Female-Led Relationship!" we'd probably feel like there was more homework to do. The fact that she can observe me serving her to her satisfaction and honoring her every wish without other people straining their necks to catch a glimpse is probably what makes our FLR beautiful.

Complete Honesty in a FLR Is Our Greatest Treasure

My wonderful Lady stresses to me the importance of total honesty if we are to regard ourselves as truly living and thriving in a special relationship based upon her accepting the huge responsibility of being my leader and my primary educator. I keep nothing from her. If she questions me, I answer truthfully - always. She cannot hope to successfully guide me through life with her feminine wisdom if I am being evasive, deceptive, telling her half-truths or outright lies.

One of the lovely things about a FLR, which maybe sets it apart from some other kinds of relationships, is that it can really only work if there is complete 2-way honesty (or, in our case, 3-way). If one of the partners is any way untrue, it's questionable whether they're really living a FLR. Ultimately it's self-defeating and the relationship will come unstuck. I could tell a lie to my Lady today and it's possible she would believe it. Maybe again tomorrow. Eventually I would drop straight into the very deep hole I'd dug for myself and there'd be very little point in her wasting her time to show me a way out of it. She has taught me that she can only lead me and show me the power of the Feminine Divine if I am open to her and lay my soul bare at her feet. That is my motivation and what I work towards daily.

It took great patience on my Lady's part to lead me safely to a place where I could be absolutely open and honest with her. She alerted me to the fact early on that should my trust in her ever be less than a hundred per cent she wouldn't be able to help me and we might as well say goodbye. It was clear that she could never abide a servant who tried to airbrush his thoughts and feelings from his intuitive Domina. It's confronting at first. There was no point deceiving either her or myself. If, in her absence, I neglected to attend to one of her directives with proper diligence, I needed to reflect on that ... and tell her. She matches her forgiveness with my eagerness to learn and improve.

We Never Called It a Female Led Relationship...But It Was

Carla and I started dating in the mid-1980s. It was a blind date set up by a mutual friend that had known me since our early teens and worked with Carla at a business in midtown Manhattan. Our first date was at the Metropolitan Museum of Art.

We met in the early afternoon. My first impression was she had a great smile and was striking to look at and assertive in conversation to say the least. She walked with purpose and held her head even. She was both humble and confident. She knew what she wanted. Her voice was steady and articulate.

She liked the fact that I asked good questions which meant I was listening, so we began sharing our philosophies, love of art, social and political leanings, and so forth. Our conversation lasted it seemed over five hours and included a small dinner and a glass of wine. She asked me whether I was doing anything the next night and so we made a date. It blossomed from there.

The second, third and fourth dates we talked even deeper about our desires and in the process we had extended hours of foreplay. She said she felt most comfortable being in control and at one point said to me that if we become more serious that my penis would belong to her and I would only be loyal to her. I accepted it as an experiment. Upon hearing that, she said I was a good boy and we made love.

I realized she was training me through empathy, support, and affirmation. Her open mind was powerful. She was intelligent and well read. She enchanted me. The unique thing about it was how natural it felt. Her direction was more like mentoring.

I'm not a macho person. And she was looking for someone intelligent that also enjoyed reading, film and music. The more we discussed, the more she wanted to guide me. She inquired about little things in my life and I found I wanted to be supportive of her. She didn't ask but I found myself buying her earrings and flowers and helping her in the selection of lingerie and high heels. She asked me after helping her buy one pair of high heels if I had ever given a pedicure and said she loved having her feet pampered. I then learned how to give a pedicure.

Essential to developing our relationship was chemistry – physically, spiritually and intellectually. Carla's natural take-charge attitude was both nurturing and matter a fact. She cultivated her dominance without explicitly saying I am going to do this or that because I'm dominant. That would have been false for her. She cultivated my natural desire to serve her and I in turn supported her natural desire to lead. We fed into each other's nature. It was erotic. We got married about six months after our first date and with the understanding of each our respective roles. The marriage lasted over 17 years until her passing.

We never used the words female led relationship. Still, that's essentially what it was. I enjoyed cooking, cleaning and loved waiting on her. I like my homes to be organized and she would request that I only wear an apron while I cleaned and cooked.

I really enjoyed giving her massages and if I got home before her I would put together an appetizer and pour a glass of wine. I remember many occasions she would open the door and I could hear from her sighs that she had another rough day. She would sit on our couch and ask me to come over to her and kneel in front of her, offering her pleasure. It was her way of unwinding and also mine.

She liked wearing business suits that were oriented to pinstripe along with ankle strapped heels. She liked feeling sexy. I would help her get dressed especially if she went out for the evening with her friends, both female and male. My work entailed a lot of paper work and so I didn't mind her evenings out. A happy wife is a happy life is an old saying but true. Indeed it was. We both knew when she returned I would be there for her.

We regularly shared our secrets, fantasies, hopes, desires and issues. We were not free of issues but talked to each other about those issues - that were mostly work and money related. As a couple it seemed easy compared to our friends that had children. We decided from the beginning that we didn't want children but just wanted to enjoy each other's company, try to do reasonably well in our careers and be part of what we considered worthwhile causes.

Over the years we explored and experimented with what was erotic and varied our routines, and about eleven years into the marriage after watching a foreign film about a woman that had a man on side on a semi-regular basis…we discussed it and experimented with it on a number of occasions. We talked about issues of potential jealousy related concerns and worked through whatever those concerns might be.

There were times I was there with her so that we both experienced the encounter. Other times I wasn't there. She experimented with both men and women. I remember more than a few times bathing and massaging her when she returned home or was finished with an encounter and then laying naked in each other's arms afterwards and talking about it. It was hot. Her exploration added balance to our relationship, reducing my stress to perform and it heightened our love for each other.

I Found My FLR While at Work

I suppose that I have always fantasized about being with a dominant woman, but it was about five years ago that I started to read about FLR and to begin to understand that there was much more to it. A few years back, I did hire a pro domme for a couple of three hour sessions. I liked being submissive but something was missing. I wanted more, to be friends, partners. I knew that I wanted to find someone who was into this lifestyle, and hopefully we would develop a long term relationship, fall in love. Call me a hopeless romantic. I had no idea how hard a task it would be to find someone. That was why what you wrote about dating in a vanilla world and finding someone, well, it really hit home with me.

Searching on the websites geared to D/s was not the answer. I basically gave up looking. I first met Lee when I was handling a legal matter for her. We kept everything on a professional lawyer/client basis. I am older than her, but, I guess I did not do a very good job of hiding the fact that I was very attracted to her. Me trying to be discreet and all business, but stealing a glance, noticing her perfume, what she was wearing. Anyway, after her case was over, I lost touch with her for about a year.

One day, I was on yahoo messenger, which was something I hardly ever do. Lee was online, and out of the blue, sent me a request to accept her contact. In our first chat, she was almost angry with me, asking me why I had never kept in contact. I think I responded with "sorry" and it was almost a week before we chatted again. To be honest I was not even sure who I was talking to at first and it took me sometime just to figure out who it was. The contact request was from Ashley, finally it clicked that Ashley was my former client Lee.

So, fast forward we talked a lot before meeting and dating. One day, I decided to pour my feelings out and tell her how I felt - I ended up writing the following email and after she read it, she said it really touched her heart.

Dear Ashley: With the aid of lifting parts of some articles that I have read on the subject, I have decided to write down what I believe to be true about the subject of female superiority in general. There is what is called a FLR or Female Led Relationship. I believe that Women are naturally more intelligent, as well as much more logical, and obviously more nurturing and Dominant than any man could ever try to be. A Woman can enter a room easily. Her entrance is noted by everyone therein. She has her beauty and natural grace.

For the most part, males still do not equal the power, wisdom, or intelligence that any Woman has. Men are raised and groomed to be very prideful creatures, which often gets in the way of 'real' thinking. The usual joke about men not wanting to stop and ask for directions is a perfect example. Men do not want to think of themselves as 'less' than they build themselves up to be in their own minds. Beyond that, look at the miracle of childbirth. This is something that Women have done since the dawn of time… and they survive it generally, and are able to do it again and again.

Men are inferior in the fact that not only do they NOT have the ability to give birth… they could not endure the pain involved, nor do they have the responsibility to care for the offspring (as mentioned above).Women's bodies are so much more complex and detailed than men's bodies. This is the biological proof of their perfection. Much more effort is put into their forms, so therefore, men should ideally worship this perfect form. Beyond the biological, there is the physical as well.

Women traditionally have been made into beautiful works of art. Paintings and sculptures throughout the centuries have all been highly regarded, and the majority of them are appreciated, because they are representations of the perfect being… a Woman. This is another way Women are far superior to men, just in their beauty and the efforts they put in to maintain this perfection. Women will be artists as they apply makeup, however a man is far too lazy and arrogant to ever consider anything like this. A man will be lucky if he washes his face and shaves. But Women can spend time perfecting their 'art' over the years of their life, and create such soft smooth features by arranging the right lines and colors and textures along the pallet of their features, easily accentuating what is already there.

Women also will endure everything from complex garments, including heels, pantyhose/stockings, corsets, garters, bras and other finely developed outfits, all to enhance the beauty they possess. I love knowing you are willing to wear such things for me Ashley. As a general rule, men once again prove their laziness by not bothering to make more of an effort than jeans or shorts and shirt. The simple fact is males in general have no concept of how to properly dress themselves.

One of the biggest problems males have, is simply the amount of testosterone in their bodies. Again, Women have a much more complex balance of hormones, but men simply have too much. With all this testosterone in their bodies, it makes them much more aggressive and brutal in general. Basically a man is almost always 'looking' for a fight or an argument. Some men are able to temper these feelings and have been trained to behave to live in modern society, but in general, many wars, brawls, and altercations would have been prevented if Women were simply to keep males in check and on a tight leash. I know that growing up, I would have been a much better behaved male in a Female dominated society.

Ashley, I am so very lucky to have finally found you and you are such a strong powerful intelligent and beautiful woman. It will be exciting to discuss and explore this adventure that will be a part of our marriage. I have a strong feeling that together we will grow and go deeper into this, all the while making it a very loving adventure. You prove beyond a shadow of a doubt, that women are superior. And what about my submission to you? I am really not sure where I would be categorized regards my submission. Perhaps I fall, I think, to some degree into every category. I do know that I am eager to explore all facets of my submissive side with your help. With you, I am willing to discuss and explore it all and allow you to push my limits.

Well like I admitted, I have never before dared to share these thoughts with anyone. It seems so easy and comfortable to talk with you, and the thought of us being together, as husband and wife, well I honestly am very pleased and happy to share this with you.

Love always, Jim

I would encourage any male, who is interested in being a partner with a Powerful Woman, to open up and see if that woman he is dating might be receptive to all this. We are planning on getting married, building a new house and having a special room outfitted. Needless to say I am very happy.

I Gain Strength from Demonstrating Obedience

I wanted to express a few feelings and sentiments regarding the often contentious issues of 'obedience' and 'polyandry' within the context of a committed FLR. As it happens, both of these ideas work well for us and have contributed to our mutual love and respect but they are not easy concepts to embrace nor are they one dimensional. They are multi-layered and there is sub-text to them. The cold clinical definitions are probably not enough to sustain a long-term FLR and to search for the delights to be discovered in their deeper meaning probably requires time and patience. A lot of it.

Obedience, for example, goes far beyond command and obey. It can be that but, for us at least, it's probably a whole lot more. My Lady encourages me to discuss most things with her, sometimes for days, and to offer my opinions where appropriate. I do all I can to help her arrive at the best decision. Once made, her decision is final and she expects and appreciates my immediate attentiveness. I want to honor her wishes. She understands, accepts and nurtures my belief in the formidable power of her feminine intelligence and thus takes her leadership role seriously and conscientiously. She regards my obedience to her as a precious gift, one she likes to have on display.

We are a triad of sorts. My Lady has a devoted lover who is much younger than myself and who continues to be an increasingly important part of our lives. Although I certainly accept that this kind of 3-way relationship isn't going to work for everybody, it has been a blessing for us. It has enabled her to express herself creatively as a sensual confident woman and to enjoy being the Goddess to her attentive 'boys'.

I'm not sure if it makes me a cuckold or not, the definition has always been unclear to me. We don't have a 3-way sexual relationship, in fact we males don't see each other very often. Her lover lives a short distance away. When she wants to be with him he will usually come here and collect her, they'll go out then back to his place. Occasionally they will come back here and she'll direct me to sleep in the spare room. She has led me to appreciate the complexities of her needs and emotions, the importance of keeping them close to my heart and soul and how best to utilize all that she has taught me in order to become a better servant to her.

Also, I gain great strength - spiritually, emotionally and otherwise - from demonstrating my complex obedience to her infinitely more complex, intelligent and articulate directives, wishes and mere whims, and from seeing her natural dominance over me bloom so beautifully each time she embraces her lover in my presence.

My FLR Does Not Involve Sexual Control

I am involved in a Female Led Relationship that does not use sexual control. I love self-pleasure and would be miserable if I didn't do it several times a day. That in no way diminishes the absolute love, adoration and respect that I have for my girlfriend and she does not see it as a problem that she has to correct.

Honestly I think I would feel less eager to serve my beautiful girlfriend if I was deprived of my self-pleasure or was in chastity. I serve her because I love her, I genuinely want her to feel strong and powerful. I want her to get her way. My support is a beautiful gift to her, at least that is how I view it. I always seek to please her. I feel absolutely awful about myself if I screw something up and make her unhappy. For me this all comes from a place of total love and respect.

I want her to be in control of the relationship. I need her to be in control of the relationship. I absolutely worship the ground she walks on, and it feels so good to me to make her feel special and powerful by always putting her needs first and deferring to her if there is ever any type of disagreement.

So I definitely do not think one requires sexual control for a successful FLR. There just needs to be a true desire on the part of the man to empower and please the woman. As far as my motivation for my support, I am motivated by my love for her. We don't really have any set repercussions for bad service. When she's unhappy I feel like total shit, and that's worse than any made up punishment could make me feel. I never want to let her down.

Perhaps our relationship is an outlier. We have had an on again off again relationship for about 5 years. We've experimented with a lot of things, from a traditional relationship, to switching roles in a D/s (we are both switches). We always had a lot of conflict and miscommunication and it got messy.

Then I stumbled across the concept of FLR and presented it to her. I told her honestly that it became clear to me that I could never end this relationship because I just love her too damn much, and that I was going to accept everything she did and not try to control her anymore. We butted heads a lot.

I vowed to her that her needs would always come first from that point on. That she made the final decision about everything. That she can do whatever the fuck she wanted to do, period, and I would embrace it. I told her she now makes the rules, and while I might want to discuss something from time to time at the end of the day she makes the rules and she has final say.

That was about 6 months ago, and things have never been better between us. It took all the conflict out of our relationship. It took all the pressure off of her. She can do anything she wants to and I will unconditionally love her, support her and obey her. It's such a beautiful concept, I feel so lucky to have stumbled across it. I wish more men could be secure enough about themselves to give it a try.

A Good Man Deserves Appreciation

As a woman in a Loving Female Led Relationship you might be tempted to start feeling entitled or "spoiled" for lack of better words. I get this way sometimes. My husband normally shows no sign of being upset by it so it had become something I didn't even realize.

There was one incident where he brought home some Subway sandwiches. He usually knows exactly how I want my sandwich and of course I'm a little picky. I forgot what he ordered on the sandwich but I just remember the sandwich was wrong and I was just like, "Oh, NOOOO... I don't want this! How could you get this for me, you know I don't eat this!?" Most people would have said, "Oh, well you better eat it anyway," because it really wasn't that serious but he went all the way back to Subway and got me another sandwich. He said, "Man, you are so spoiled." That made me stop and think.

Ladies, we have to start appreciating our men more and not taking his way of loving and supporting us for granted. This man is willing to do ANYTHING that will make you happy and satisfied and that takes a lot of courage and love in this day and age. He must not feel that he is being taken advantage of or used even if he gives you the opportunity to do that.

Female Led Relationships are such a beautiful thing in a world where the happiness and opinion of women is often a non-factor. But, in my home it's my world, thanks to my husband. My world would be NOTHING without the love, support and admiration from my husband. You have to find ways to show him appreciation. I buy my husband gifts a lot out of the blue and "just because."

Sometimes it is a shirt with his favorite Rapper on it, a very bright LCD flashlight that he can use when working on his truck or his favorite food made when he comes home from work even though I feel he shouldn't be eating that way. And don't forget the occasional blow-job, just to show that you care and make him feel special. My husband also knows I will go to WAR for him.

Because I know that he is passive, I am very protective of him. FLR's are not about just kicking back and getting served. There is much responsibility on the part of the female to be the type of woman that can handle taking the lead.

He Wants To Be the Source of My Happiness

I always wondered why people pressure the man to be the leader of the relationship especially because of religion. What if the woman in the relationship is just better at leading? Why force it on the man if this is not something he does not have a desire to do?

My husband made my happiness the top priority and he allows me to direct the relationship. It was about what I wanted and not about what he wanted for me. I dominate the arguments. Most of the time he just sits and listens and doesn't really try to resist or argue with me. Not saying that he doesn't express his opinions, but he just has no desire to argue with me about anything.

Upon us first starting the relationship he always wanted to pamper me. It started with him never wanting me to "have to work." Of course if I am working because I want to he supports it, but he never wanted to place me in a position where I *have* to work to make ends meet.

He also did not like to sit back while I did house work or things like that. He wanted me to be the one sitting back and relaxing while he does those things. Everything I ask him to do he would does it or tries his best to get done. He trusts me not to take advantage of him in a negative way, but he wanted me to use him to my advantage if that makes sense.

When it comes to our budget, he is the bread winner, but I am in charge of what we do with the money and I have done a great job so far. When we moved to Houston there was time when he had to get a car title loan and pawn a lot of our belongings, but now we have a good amount in savings. All our bills are paid on time and we have much left over to have some fun with. We have goals and ambitions.

He always looked for my approval on things and made sure I was happy. I have made all the major decisions in our relationship. I made the choice for us to move from a small east Texas city to Houston Texas. I am making the decision for us to move to a smaller suburb outside of Houston when our lease is up where we live. We can still work in Houston and enjoy the exciting things that the city offers without all the clutter and complications of city life.

The things that he is in charge of, I put him in charge of those things. He does all the things willingly that I can't do like car and house maintenance. When we go out together he does the driving, because he is the better driver in this huge city. I let him lead on things publicly when I feel that it will cause people to respect us more. Like when we have went car shopping, he looks at the cars and talks to the salesmen and makes sure the car is in good running condition and that we are getting a fair deal, but when it comes to the paper work I come in and take charge. I have the brains and he has the brawn I guess.

When it comes to Spirituality he follows my lead and trusts me. We started out as Christians and I was a very important part of my church and he supported me every step of the way. This is where it was first brought to my attention that men are supposed to rule the household and they are the spiritual leaders. But if you are better at doing that than the man, why is this something that would be forced? Why can't the better person just do it?

At the time I had even made a choice that we should be celibate and we were for about 7 months. When I started to become more enlightened and ended up leaving the church and started seeking answers on my own, he followed my lead on that as well and trusted me. I am someone who always wants the truth no matter what and I am honest and forthcoming with him and he admires that.

He wanted to be the source of my happiness. He wanted everyone to see how he takes care of me, how he provides for me and does everything for me without me lifting a finger. This has not always been a perfect situation because I didn't respect him like I should because I felt he should be more dominant because that is what society tells us. I considered him to be "p***y whipped."

On a serious note I am just the more responsible one. Not taking anything away from him, it is just that when you compare us, I am more the more responsible and organized one. I think he just noticed that in me and feels like I am better at leading the household than he would be, so why not let me do what I am already great at doing. I don't think it was anything intentional of me leading the household it's just the way it came to be when our personalities came together.

Since discovering your website and reading the different stories I am starting to admire and respect him for who he is and what he is trying to give to me. It is really making our relationship better and I feel closer to him in this aspect.

I Am the Ultimate Decision Maker

Imagine being in bed with your lover who does everything you mandate as soon as you state your desire. He is skilled at bringing your repeated orgasms during a long lovemaking session without ever climaxing himself or asking for release. When you are physically and mentally exhausted, he rubs your back and neck or drops to his knees and messages your feet upon your command. If you regain your energy, you call him back and he is looking into your eyes as you have him make love to you for as long as you want.

Even important, your partner is your best friend and continues that level of service outside your bedroom. He focuses on you and your pleasure, follows your commands without delay or attitude. He works to anticipate your needs and exceed them. Best yet, he has learned to be obedient, to take criticism as a way to better serve you and please you – and, thus, add to his life.

Yes, this approach is part of what some people call FLR – Female Led Relationships. For others, their sex life is not included in the FLR; some FLRs could have vanilla sex lives. What matters is that the female is the leader and the male relies on her leadership and decision making within the boundaries that work for them. Each FLR is individually established.

Communications and setting parameters that works for the couple is central for the success of the individual relationship. One might argue that FLRs takes a far higher level of communications, although some people would view that once the ground rules are established, all other decisions are easier since one person is ultimately in charge.

As a couple who have read considerably on FLRs and met with other couples in a FLR and/or Femdom relationship, we realize relationships are very different, even if they are under the umbrella of FLR. Beyond the kink that will be explained below, a major portion of this approach is a focus on the lady. The man is not usually considered to be inferior by either partner. This is not the case in all FLRs; in some, the basis is that the man *is* inferior. That is not the case with us.

Yet, in a FLR, the gentleman is giving of himself in ways that do not occur in other long-term relationships. In the case of a FLR, the woman ultimately makes the decisions, although she will often listen to her mate's thoughts, many times take into consideration of his wants and true needs. She will do things that are special for him including some activities she may not enjoy at times (attending a baseball game or giving head). These activities are not regularly given but can be a special reward or gift to him. I decide. While we communicate about what is working and what might not work as well. I am the ultimate decision maker.

I Want You to Have Absolute Control

I am with a woman now who is naturally controlling, has said she is and I don't fight it. But, it's inconsistent, not outright. What I desire or need is absolute control of me and absolute freedom for her. I recently wrote something but haven't given it to her.

Tish, this is for you:

1. Finances: Money/Pay/Rent/Any other sources — Tisha (all monetary decisions are yours in the event we don't or can't agree. This means that our relationship is more along the lines of, "This is what I'm planning on doing, what do you think Paul?"

— I already agreed to give control of my money to you and you have yours as well. I also agreed to abide by your decisions without complaint or argument. What I'm asking is that you do this with intention and not change or make exceptions. I am okay with you having control of this. I want it and equally important I need it, even if sometimes I may want something now. It doesn't matter what I want and I'm asking you to be firm and just tell me, please don't ask, that you made your decision and that's it. Remind me that I gave you this control and wanted you to have it, coupled with the fact that you want to control finances. An example is the $100 I asked for. I did not use it for the reason you gave it to me. I should have given it back as soon as I got back to the car. If I didn't, I want and need for you tell me, not ask, to give it back to you. Had I returned it we wouldn't be out of money now. I'm okay, great, actually, with you, Tisha, having complete control of ALL finances. So, you own it. Do what you think is best. I'll never question you, and honestly, if I ever do, I hope you will stop me immediately and remind me who controls the finances and that should be the end of it. Please don't cave in. I'm guessing after one time like this, you won't. You're strong and this empowers you even more, and it makes me happy knowing that.

I want to title the truck to you. This makes sense to me. If you want to control the finances, and I want you to control them, then you have to have control of the vehicles. Then you will have complete control of ALL finances and that's a good thing for us both. You want it, are good at it and I want to give it you, and this finishes it. It will make for zero conflict in anything involving money, and that covers pretty much every facet of life. I'm giving you this and agreeing up front to abide by your decisions without arguing or even complaining. I've never done anything remotely close to this, but I've always wanted to. You are the first woman I've ever known and trusted who is strong enough for me to want to give you such control. I do want to and I want you to use it. I am giving it to you, so use it without any guilt or regret. It's what I want you to do.

2. Life Direction: this would be jobs, partying, renters, moral quandaries, driving with no license, drinking, drugs, how we put our house together, vacations or anything we do now that has long term effects.

As it stands, I mostly defer to you on pretty much all of this, but not all the time. Your judgement has never been questioned by me. Only the fact that I really wanted to do something was the reason I did it even though you didn't want me to and that's not sound reasoning or good judgement. It's selfish and reckless. Driving without a license is big one, drinking, even beer is another, drugs and pretty much any other obviously bad choice made only to make me happy for a minute.

So, basically you already control this too, you just don't exercise that control all the time. Maybe you think I'd get mad or upset or feel like I don't get to have fun. I don't know. However, like I said I've never questioned what you've said about anything. I will happily give up ALL control of this too. No arguments and no complaints. I'm agreeing right now to abide by whatever you decide for whatever reason, with not even a hint of protest. So you can again exercise this control with an absolutely clear conscience. I'm giving it to you and I want you to use it. Should I ever object, remind me why you're making the decision, and say it with no uncertain terms. I'll understand completely and it's highly unlikely to occur again, if it ever does in the first place.

3. My Free Time: Haven't really thought about this in specific terms, but it's influenced heavily by the first two, Finances and Life Direction.

I pretty much ask you as it is before I do anything. Like asking if it was okay to give Chris a ride and you just flat said no and I said okay. So I guess it has been happening by default instead of design, but the result is the same. I don't know that I've ever argued about it. Since this inevitably involves money and probably some or maybe many moral and legal things, it is only sensible for you to decide this. I will give you control of this, my free time, gladly. And I want you to control it, it will be good for me and eliminate more possibility for conflict. I am agreeing now to abide by your decisions without argument or complaint. Again, if I ever do, remind me in no uncertain terms why you are making the decision.

4. Household Chores: You like things a very specific way. You will have to decide what you want to do and what you want me to do. I will do any or all. If they need to be done an exact, certain way and you want me to do it, you'll have to show me how you want it done and I will do it that way. Just tell me which chores you want me to do. The overriding reason is my desire and need to make you happy and your life easy, so on this I want to do them how you like them. So I'm giving any control I had of this to you, just decide and tell me what you want me to do.

5. Sex: I've already given you control of this, you've said we aren't having any. So this one is already completely controlled by you. I haven't argued, and I'm agreeing now that I won't, nor will I complain and I will stop the passive aggressive behavior and won't do it anymore.

When I put all of this in writing everything we discussed from the beginning becomes more clear. A majority of all of this was already there. Somehow on some things I balked. I usually caught myself and told you, but I think for both of us, it might have been difficult to keep up with what was said over the course of many conversations. So now it's crystal clear. I have said from the start that I have an overwhelming desire and even need to make you happy, to please you and make your life easy. I get all the pleasure I need by simply doing that. I don't expect or even want you to feel somehow that you should reciprocate. The whole point for me is that this is all about you. I absolutely mean that. If you are happy, pleased and life gets easier and easier, I will be happy and find new ways to make you more happy. If you think of something, no matter what it is, tell me and I'll do it or if it's something you want to do then just tell me you're doing it. I want you to be the happiest woman and it doesn't matter what it takes for that. It's all I want to spend my life doing. I want you to know that you are the center of my universe and that my purpose is you and your happiness, no matter what it is that you desire.

With such complete control you now have the means to get rid of what causes you stress and create an atmosphere that allows you to do whatever you please to make yourself happy. You are free to do absolutely anything. I'm here to do whatever you want me to and nothing that you don't. There is nothing on Earth that I wouldn't do. So you say what you want and if you want it I'll do it. You are making the decisions, you are free to do anything you want, you are totally liberated and have someone now who is there only for you and your desires.

I have agreed not to argue or complain so you have no need or reason to explain anything, no matter what you do or where you do it. You have said so many times that you need to be in control and now you really are. I feel nothing but good doing this and want you to know that I have no reservations about it. I've always wanted to be in this position and now I am. I've given you unconditional control and asked for nothing in return, save that I want you to exercise this control without hesitation. We will have a harmonious relationship with zero conflict no matter what. It's about how we started, it's just really clear now that it's written.

The Challenge Has Been to Shed My Macho Ego

I live in Washington state, just South of Seattle. I like to hike, exercise, read, play board games, socialize and be of service to the fair gender. My first girl/lady friend is an Alpha person, both in the bedroom and outside. I was initially stubborn in my macho ways and insisted on the being the 'boss' in our relationship. Thank Goddess she overpowered me with her stronger personality...I was now beta to her Alpha.

Yes, now that I see FLR relationships around me, and see that it a valid way to have and maintain a relationship, I am very accepting of the FLR. In fact I've gotten to the point where I believe it to be the natural way for the sexes to relate. We should be living in a Gynarchy to maximize who we are as humans.

The challenge has been to shed my petty, tyrannical, and macho ego. I have now to come to realize that in a relationship a woman may have greater intelligence, or greater personal strength/authority than I do and it is now quite okay. More than okay, it's actually now a pleasure to serve the woman I love.

I'm single right now so I'm hoping to be in a relationship where I can cater to Milady's happiness. I give one hell of a good massage; and I find that women really like both the healing and sensual pleasure that massage produces. I'm also no stranger to housework, chores, and running errands for the woman I am devoted to.

I wish someone had taught me that women must always be respected, and listened to respectfully. Also that women should be deferred to and treated with kindness and a willingness to do as I am now doing.

My Husband Now Enjoys Putting My Needs First

I am a Housewife. I take care of two kids, do all the cooking and clean the house, run kids to activities and have little time to myself. I was talking to a girlfriend that accidentally started bragging about her Loving Female Led Relationship after too many drinks one night. I was jealous and intrigued. I brought up the topic over time with my husband indirectly and he ended up asking me if I'd be interested in taking more control in our relationship. I slow played it as if I needed to think about it and eventually agreed to try gradually testing some scenarios.

Life is more balanced towards me, my satisfaction and happiness and my husband has less tension and pressure to be everything in our relationship. The biggest benefit is seeing how much happier he is and in turn how blessed I am to make more decisions and take control.

I'm already encouraged to flirt more while in public, dress sexier and occasionally have girls nights out with my crazier single friends that I haven't been out with much before establishing our Loving FLR. It is amazing how my husband now enjoys putting my needs first and genuinely making that a daily reality, even if it would embarrass other husbands to do the same.

I Feared That Real-Life Working FLRs May Be Imaginary

've been divorced for a few years and I live alone in a rural area outside a very small town. It's ideal for me, because I love the outdoors, especially hiking, kayaking, and mountain biking. I have three grown sons who each live about two hours away, and I try to spend time with them frequently. I work in the Internet field as a software engineer. But my dream is to downsize my career to do more writing, which is my first love. Oh, and I'm saving and planning for my next move, which will be a tiny house on wheels!

Since my teens, it seemed most natural to me to follow my partner's lead. I eventually married a very intelligent, strong-willed woman. Even before marriage, I was open with her about my orientation but she was never comfortable with the concept of an FLR. Still, we stayed married for over 20 years. The experience taught me how important it is to know myself, and to stay true to myself. I projected certain qualities onto my partner that I wanted her to have. I harbored a belief that I could somehow convince her that an FLR would be a good fit for us. I'm much more willing now to eschew partners who are not a good fit for me.

I'm encouraged to know that many other people have created FLRs that fit their needs. Not so long ago, I feared that real-life working FLRs may be imaginary, or at least impossibly rare. I no longer feel resigned to a choice between either compromising my needs or remaining alone.

I've only been in one explicit FLR thus far. The main benefit was that I could relax and relate in a way that feels natural to me, without needing to conform to a socially expected role. That felt tremendously liberating. The biggest challenge was ensuring I was not sacrificing my own needs, thus "selling myself out" in service of my partner and the relationship. For me, it requires a higher-than-average level of open communication to maintain healthy balance in a hierarchical partnership.

I was on a weekend date with my partner, staying at an AirBnB rental in a small town. She sent me out late at night, in the rain, with a list of a few unusual things she wanted, and gave me 30 minutes to find them. I don't think she expected me to succeed, but the look on her face when I returned with her items was priceless!

I'm single. I am hoping to be part of a relationship structure in which I'm loved and appreciated in a supporting role, allowing us both to thrive. Unfortunately, some people enter hierarchical relationships in order to compensate for their own insecurities, and perhaps seek to meet their own unexpressed needs at their partner's expense. So it's important that my partner is kind, compassionate, emotionally secure, and a skilled communicator.

I wish someone had told me how important it is to follow one's own inner voice. I wish someone had told me that the socially prevailing relationship models simply don't work for everyone. I wish someone had told me that it's better to live authentically than to settle for a relationship that doesn't fit. And that there exist many potentially compatible partners in the real world.

My Girlfriend is Naturally Powerful

I am a single father living in the Philadelphia area. I work in the corporate sphere and most of my enjoyment involves being a dad...going to games and doing things with my children. My girlfriend does NOT live with me at this time.

We were introduced to FLR after a breakup. As I was trying to understand why a seemingly great relationship was failing, I stumbled upon the concept of FLR. As soon as I read about it, it was obvious to me that we were perfect candidates.

My girlfriend is naturally powerful. What I learned is that I was fighting her natural authority. FLR addressed this issue in a very clear manner. I was nervous sharing this with her as I thought she would see it as some weird 'kink'. Instead, she immediately embraced it and worked as hard as I did to draft our contract.

We Don't Argue Over Stupid Things Anymore

My girlfriend and I were together for over 10 years before we embraced a FLR. Since we have signed our agreement and accepted our roles in our relationship, things have never been better. The act of simply submitting to her authority has changed everything. We don't fight, we 'talk' about things and we follow our agreement. My girlfriend is empowered and loves being 'the boss'. She has told me many times it always frustrated her I would argue over things, only to lose the argument. Now, there are no arguments. She dictates how she wants things done and that's how things are done. For me, I love that we don't argue over stupid things anymore.

The biggest benefit has been that we have developed a renewed respect for each other. She is impressed that her man would willingly give up a typical male role for the purpose of simply making her happy. She has said this many times. For me, I love that my woman is happy being the boss.

My girlfriend and I were out to dinner one night and the waitress was just over the top attractive. She caught me looking at her more than once but never said a word. When we got home she asked me to come in the bedroom. I assumed sex was imminent but instead she had me sit on the bed and proceeded to lecture me on my behavior at dinner. She expressed that it bothered her that I would look at another woman when we have a contract that clearly states my life goal is her happiness.

"Do you think it made me happy for you to look at the waitress?" she asked. It really began to sink in how seriously she took all of this and that I was completely wrong in my actions. I genuinely felt bad for the way I behaved and my apology to her was probably the most sincere in our long relationship. And at that moment, I felt very proud to be in a Loving FLR.

I wouldn't say my girlfriend has OCD but she is a control freak. When things go her way, she is awesome to be around and very happy. When things don't, she is quite difficult to tolerate. It was the source of many of our arguments for years. The day I signed our agreement and decided to stop fighting her authority, everything got better. And to this day, it continues to be great.

The biggest thing people have to get away from is the notion that a Loving FLR is some kind of kink or BDSM lifestyle. The truth is, it is exactly what you both agree it is. For my girlfriend and I, the majority of our interaction is like any other couple. We do the same things as other couples and we have the same fun. There are no whips and chains. I am not a gimp or a wimp. I am her man who acts like a man to her. I guess my point is that a Loving FLR is not a kin' to us. Yes, I am lectured and given punishments sometimes but it's not that often and it's only done when I screw up. I control my own destiny.

I Need a Strong Woman That I Can Look Up To

I know that 72 is really old but I am quite attractive and many women would be proud to be seen with me. I retired and moved from the Midwest to Tucson ten years ago to care for my then infant granddaughter. Of course she is a 10-year-old now, with a 6-year-old sister. I still drive to their house every school day morning, feed them, and drive them to their charter school. After school, I drive them home, feed and tutor them. They are excelling in both academics and athletics. Their parents, my daughter and son-in-law, are both incredibly busy doctors, so by doing this, I relax their workload. Plus I enjoy doing it I hike or go to the gym almost daily. I also enjoy camping, and there are some spectacular camping areas in Arizona.

I came across FLRs on the internet. My reaction was "Oh my God, (although I'm not really religious) this is the way I want and need it!" I admit that strong women intimidate me, yet I need a strong woman that I can look up to. Someone to give me guidance and someone whose life's burdens I could ease by basically doing the role of a supportive housewife. I keep a clean house and I enjoy cooking. Oh, and I wouldn't be a money drain on her.

The biggest benefit of a FLR is having the quality leadership of a strong woman. I will always defer to her decision making. That doesn't mean that I wouldn't counter her ideas with different suggestions, but she'd make the final decision and I would comply. The biggest challenge so far is lack of confidence in finding her.

Here's my advice to women entertaining the thought of a Loving FLR. I'm sure you remember from history that for a time women did not have the right to vote. The household had one vote. So if it were still that way, and I voted for Trump, our household has it Trump 1/ Clinton 0. But now days women have the right to vote, so make it Trump 1/ Clinton 1. Okay, in a FLR she can ask me to vote for Clinton and I will obey her. Now our household vote count is Clinton 2/ Trump 0. So strong women have come from having no vote, to those women in a FLR who now have two votes.

We Are Dependent and Admit We Need Each Other

'm a 47 year old woman. I work full-time in a management position for a non-profit. I live with my almost 13 year old daughter and am having a FLR with a man who is in the process of disengaging from a long marriage. I love going out for dinner and drinks, going to the movies and playing mini-golf, going for drives and sight-seeing, listening to music, and cooking/baking. I'm also very involved in my church.

Two years ago I divorced from the father of my child. I went online and started chatting with men and discovered that I was not the submissive woman I had thought I was, but that the relationship I was in put me in that position. I met a man who was everything I was looking for and vice-versa. We both realized that we fit the role of him being the supportive partner and me being the leader. I began reading about BDSM relationships from the femdom side of things and then learned about FLR and that clicked for us.

We've incorporated the FLR idea with our lifestyle. He needs to please me in every way. He cherishes and worships me and needs to prove that he does. I seek the reassurance that he does in fact cherish me, so it keeps the cycle going. I need the affirmation and he needs to give it to me. I've also never been able to let someone pamper me - it always felt that I would become too vulnerable to "need" someone else.

In this relationship, we are dependent and admit we need each other and what the other gives us and it's become very safe (protective), loving, and open. We're completely honest with our feelings and desires and have no desire to hide anything from each other. The biggest challenge, and it's not really a challenge but an awareness, is to be sure we're doing what we honestly want to do. It's good to do these checks and we find that it's a win-win in many cases, and we're also honest saying that it scares us and we're not completely sure. We're going into the whole thing together, for US and if it doesn't make US stronger, then we won't continue. We're often monitoring where we are and if it's where we want to be, as any relationship should.

When we go out together and he wants me to select what we eat and where we go and what we do, but also knowing that if I want him to make that decision or get his input, it's because it's what I want, so essentially, it is by my lead, I feel proud of what we have and it feels special.

In any relationship, if you think you're doing something that just feels wrong or even questioning if something feels right, it's probably not what you should be doing. Listen to yourself and allow yourself to say you do not want to do whatever that is you don't feel comfortable about. Your partner should accept that. If they don't, and won't, that's not the relationship you want to be in.

VISIT US ONLINE

LovingFLR.Com

Loving FLR is the gateway to joining the Loving FLR Community. Subscribers will receive exclusive content by email and will be notified when new courses are added to our online school, coaching programs will be offered and new blog posts have been posted.

FLRStyle.Com

FLR Style is our Online Boutique for Loving Female Led Relationship Lifestyle & Fashion items like custom jewelry, t-shirts, hats and household items for men and women. It also offers access to online classes like the **Loving FLR Leadership Coaching Program**, **Loving FLR 101**, **Becoming an Anchor in a Female Led Relationship** and our **Loving FLR Interview Series**.

FLRMatchmakingService.Com

We connect Powerful Women with the Gentlemen who adore them.

WRITE A REVIEW

Thank you for reading!

If you enjoyed this collection of Loving FLR Stories please share a book review to help spread the word about Loving FLRs!

Printed in Great Britain
by Amazon